I
LOVE
OHIO STATE

STEVE GREENBERG
& DALE RATERMANN

TRIUMPH
BOOKS

Library of Congress Cataloguing-in-Publication Data
Ratermann, Dale, 1956–
    I love Ohio State, I hate Michigan / Dale Ratermann and Steve Greenberg.
        p. cm.
    ISBN 978-1-60078-578-8
    1. Ohio State University—Football—Miscellanea. 2. Ohio State Buckeyes (Football team)—Miscellanea. 3. University of Michigan—Football—Miscellanea. 4. Michigan Wolverines (Football team)—Miscellanea. 5. Sports rivalries—United States—Miscellanea. I. Greenberg, Steve, 1956– II. Title.
    GV958.O35R38 2011
    796.332'630977—dc22

                                                            2011010692

This book is available in quantity at special discounts for your group or organization. For further information, contact:

Triumph Books
542 South Dearborn Street
Suite 750
Chicago, Illinois 60605
(312) 939-3330
Fax (312) 663-3557
www.triumphbooks.com

Printed in U.S.A.
ISBN: 978-1-60078-578-8
Editorial production by Prologue Publishing Services, LLC
Photos courtesy of AP Images unless otherwise indicated

RATED M FOR MATURE

PARENTAL WARNING:
There are some naughty words in here, some from us, most from Woody Hayes quotes.

CONTENT RATED BY
S G D R

To the memories of Coach Woody Hayes and my good friends and childhood heroes, Larry Zelina and Neal Colzie. Each packed such zeal for this rivalry that it stoked my fervor to an even greater pitch. Great Buckeyes, may they rest in peace. Also to Coach John Johnson, who, for a West Virginia native, is as Scarlet and Gray as they come. —S.G.

For Sanchez J. Jiminez, my trusted associate, who provided counsel deep into the night as we wrote this book. —D.R.

CONTENTS

FOREWORD
WINNING WITH WOODY HAYES

I FIRST MET STEVE GREENBERG several years ago when I was writing my book, *Tyson-Douglas: The Inside Story*, and looking for a publisher for a first-time author. Although that book was primarily about my experience as the manager of Buster Douglas during his triumphant upset of Mike Tyson, several chapters were devoted to my time as a graduate assistant football coach at Ohio State from 1972 to 1975, during the heyday of the Woody Hayes–Bo Schembechler rivalry. As Steve and I, and coauthor Bill Long (himself a former OSU quarterback), worked on the *Tyson-Douglas* book together, we often marveled at the parallels between the two experiences. I had stood on the sideline next to Woody Hayes in college football's greatest rivalry during arguably its most memorable era. I had been in the locker room during those tense, waning moments before the Buckeyes ran out of the tunnel to face the mighty Michigan Wolverines, witnessing firsthand as Woody drove his fist into the metal lockers time after time to emphasize to everyone how much the game meant, shouting: "We are going to kick Michigan's ass!" And I had seen tears stream from the eyes of John Hicks, Archie Griffin, and Brian Baschnagel after we had beaten the "school up north" to win the Big Ten title and the Rose Bowl berth that came with it.

Fifteen years later, as Buster Douglas and I walked confidently to the ring in the Tokyo Dome as 42–1 underdogs against the ferocious, unbeatable "Iron" Mike Tyson, I could feel the intensity and hear the words of Coach Hayes (who had passed away three years earlier), which were so indelibly part of my psyche: *John, don't listen to those bastards that doubt you, who want you to lose...you and Buster have prepared for this day all of your lives. The team that hits the hardest, the longest, and makes the fewest mistakes is going to be victorious. And damn it, John, that team is going to be you!*

I had preached these words to Buster over and over during our six years as coach and athlete, and I knew he was ready to shock the world. Ten rounds later, with Tyson on his knees in front of our corner, famously grasping for his mouthpiece, I looked to the sky (actually, the ceiling of the Tokyo Dome) and with tears streaming down shouted, "Coach, we did it! We did it!" Looking back on both of these remarkable times in my life, Steve and I realized the inextricable connection between them: the second could not have happened without the first. Without my experience as a low-on-the-totem-pole graduate assistant during the OSU-Michigan rivalry, I could never have helped prepare Buster Douglas for the magnitude, intensity, and, yes, *visceral hatred* for the opponent that was necessary to pull off the greatest upset in the history of heavyweight boxing.

Now, as I look back some 20 years after Douglas-Tyson, and 35 years after my last game on the sideline at Ohio State, I realize how much The Game is still a major part of who I am. This past November, Buster and I were invited to participate in an OSU-Michigan Celebrities for Diabetes charity dinner

Woody Hayes roamed the sideline at the 'Shoe as Ohio State football's head coach from 1951 to 1978, leading the Buckeyes to 13 Big Ten titles and three national championships. Photo courtesy of Getty Images

event hosted each year by Hicks, the former OSU All-America tackle. Former players from both OSU and Michigan spoke about the meaning of the rivalry. It is always an outstanding event on the eve of The Game, and last year's event—which honored the memory of Jack Tatum—had former Michigan stars John Wangler, Jamie Morris, and Bob Thornblade representing the Maize and Blue; and William White, Tim Anderson, and Ron Maciejowski representing the Buckeyes. Each of these former greats spoke eloquently (and often humorously) about the rivalry and recounted the passion with which Hayes and Schembechler prepared for each other. During his presentation, Thornblade looked down the dais at the OSU players and said, "Gentlemen, I see White, Anderson, and Maciejowski, and I think we could take you. But then I look down and see Buster Douglas at the table, and that just isn't fair!" The comment drew quite a laugh from the crowd, and though I never played a down for either team, I felt as if I had just thrown the winning touchdown pass in the Horseshoe.

I still proudly wear my Big Ten Championship and Rose Bowl rings on one hand, and my World Heavyweight Boxing Championship ring on the other. I have three pairs of Gold Pants hanging from my neck that I cherish more and more with each passing day. When people ask me about these items, I always tell them that because of what I learned from Woody Hayes—discipline, intensity, preparation, and unfailing belief in oneself—I had no doubt that Buster Douglas would one day be heavyweight champion of the world. Buster was my personal Ohio State, wearing the white trunks with scarlet trim, representing all that was good and right in the world; Tyson, without question, was Michigan, wearing the dark trunks and representing the bitter enemy from up north.

On a shelf in my office sits a copy of Woody Hayes' book, *You Win With People*. I have it opened to display the front page, where Coach Hayes autographed it to my late father when he lay dying in the hospital. The inscription: "To Mr. Dayton Johnson—You have a son, John, of whom you can be very proud." It is one of my greatest honors and possessions. These days, as I watch the Buckeyes take the field against Michigan each year, I can't help but think there is a young graduate assistant somewhere on the sideline having the same feelings that coursed through my veins more than 35 years ago. And I know that Coach Hayes is looking down, proud that the Buckeyes coaches are out there following in his footsteps—inspiring young men and kicking Michigan's ass.

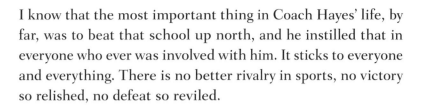

I know that the most important thing in Coach Hayes' life, by far, was to beat that school up north, and he instilled that in everyone who ever was involved with him. It sticks to everyone and everything. There is no better rivalry in sports, no victory so relished, no defeat so reviled.

One day, as I was arriving at my gym, one of my new fighters got out of his car. What I saw enraged me. The kid was wearing a sweatsuit with an *M* prominently displayed on it. I truly was beside myself. I asked him how much he paid for it, and he said it cost him $40. I gave him $100 for the sweatsuit on the spot. It had rained that day, and I took the garment, put it in a rain-filled mud puddle, and jumped up and down on it several times. I then got in my car and drove back and forth across it several times, and then I threw it in the trash. People think I'm crazy when it comes to this stuff; if you witnessed my display, that probably would confirm it for you. But I take great comfort in the fact that somewhere up above Coach Hayes was smiling down on me.

That was no act. I'm not in the habit of tossing $100 down the drain. It was purely and simply a reflection of how heated this rivalry is and how hated Michigan is around these parts. We just have to beat them every year; losing is unacceptable and distasteful. In a perfect world, Gold Pants would be the perfect season-ending gift. Every single year. Forever.

—John Johnson

INTRODUCTION
WHY WE LOVE THE BUCKEYES

You're going to Michigan? Why you dumb, no-good sonofa-bitch! You go right ahead. You go there, and when you play against Ohio State, we'll just see whether you gain a yard against us all day. We'll break you in two.

—Woody Hayes
(having lost a recruit to that school up north)

YOU'VE MORE THAN LIKELY heard or read every cliché about the Ohio State–Michigan football rivalry. Here are two, courtesy of myriad radio and television announcers down through the years: "You can throw out the record books when these two teams get together" and "What happened this season really doesn't matter to either team as long as your team wins today." As each football season dawns (does it ever have a sunset?), this game—The Game—is always a focal point because more often than not it will be a make-it-or-break-it scenario for a coach's longevity (hello, Earle Bruce, John Cooper, Lloyd Carr, Rich Rodriguez) and/or his team's postseason bowl fate. It possibly could mean more in Columbus than in Ann Arbor (that whore), where the largest cash crop is marijuana. They always want to make a point about something up there, but they, uh, forget—they *do* love Snickers dipped in organic hummus, though.

On our side, the hatred runs deep, almost as deep as that harbored by the late and very great Wayne Woodrow "Woody" Hayes. You've heard this: Woody was on a recruiting trip up north, his car was critically low on fuel, and rather than filling it up at one of "their" gas stations, he and his traveling companion, assistant coach Ed Ferkany, pushed on toward the Ohio line. Said Woody, "Keep going! I don't spend five lousy cents in the state of Michigan. We'll make it to the Ohio line if we have to get out and push." In truth, we both have purchased fuel in Michigan; we don't like to push our vehicles. Other than that, Michigan can kiss our scarlet-and-gray asses!

So when the folks at Triumph Books offered the chance to write this tome, we flashed back to our high school years. One of us lived in Columbus at the time, and he possibly... perhaps...might have...maybe could have been involved in chicanery that involved the clandestine theft from a porch of one of those butt-ugly Michigan flags belonging to some sucker with the onions to fly it. You know the one—dark blue with an upside-down *yellow* W on it. Dude had the *audacity* to fly that rag in *our* city during the week of The Game. That was a lot of years ago. It was a dark and stormy night, and empty 3.2-beer cans might have been strewn all over the front yard of a neighboring house, where a party the night before might have raged under the direction of the Clearasil crowd. We might have been getting pumped up for another clash of the titans the next day. It's very possible the blue-and-yellow flag may have been placed dead center on the pavement of a quiet, tree-lined, suburban street in Columbus that evening and had some skunky 3.2-beer poured onto it. And it's possible a certain someone with a strong connection to us backed his parents' Chrysler New Yorker onto the flag, with the rear tires just beyond the upside-down W, and repeatedly laid patches on it. When rubber met cotton, that's about all it took. It was, as they say, poetry in motion, folks.

Needless to say, the neighborhood was awakened. All H-E-double-hockey-sticks was being raised in the name of perpetrating what we know to be an impossible physical act on a despised football team and everyone associated with it. Poor flag never had a chance. The flag's owner, to our knowledge, never gathered the additional onions to fly another one. He probably packed the bowl of his Meerschaum pipe, smoothed a stray wrinkle from his cashmere cardigan, and plowed back into his fireside favorite, *What It Means to Be a Wolverine*. It's kind of like the definition of the meaning of life—no one knows.

As for we Buckeyes, yeah, we've taken our lumps in this series and trail it badly, 44–57–6, but history is rewriting itself. (Did we just write that?) Look, as we tickle the keyboards for this project, it has been well more than 2,600 days since the guys up north beat us and will be 2,919 when we play them up north on November 26, 2011. Actually, Mee-chigan has been little more than a minor bit of turbulence along a glorious Buckeyes flight in recent years. Blowouts for our side are common. We out-recruit, outcoach, and outsell them by a country mile. The tables are turning. Matter of fact, find us one with a stupid candelabra on it at a tailgate party up there, and we'll show you how they turn. It's not the friggin' symphony on the prairie, Skippy, it's *The Game*, and we own your asses these days. We'll pass on the baked brie, Merlot, and the crudités. Send over a couple brats and beers, damn it!

Now that we have clarified the back half of the book with all manner of venom spewed, let us tell you why we love Ohio State. Follow along: the Buckeye Battle Cry, Across the Field, Heisman trophies, All-Americans, Buckeye Leaves (proper noun in Columbus, as it should be), the Victory Bell (sweetest tonal quality ever), the Gold Pants (another proper noun, as it should be), Mirror Lake, Buckeye Grove, the Senior Tackle (same grammar lesson), Tunnel of Pride (ditto—this grammar crap is getting monotonous, so ride with us for just another moment, please), Captain's Breakfast, "Hang on Sloopy," Skull Session, O–HI–O, "Carmen Ohio" (who, "most definitely," as ath-a-letes would say, is *not* a whore), and Script Ohio (after this book is released, it's a dead-solid lock we'll be asked to dot the *i*), among many, many others. Patience! You're about to find out.

1

WE LOVE BEATING MICHIGAN

EVERY VICTORY AGAINST that school up north is a game we love. Sometimes an otherwise disappointing season can become worthwhile when it concludes with a thumping of the blue and yellow. But some victories are just more lovable than others—whether the game itself is simply more exciting or the drama of the situation makes the winning that much sweeter. Whatever the reason, here are the top 15 Buckeyes victories in the most storied series in college football.

No. 1: 2006

| MICHIGAN | 7 | 7 | 10 | 15 | **39** |
| OHIO STATE | 7 | 21 | 7 | 7 | **42** |

It was billed as the "Game of the Century." Undefeated and No. 1–ranked Ohio State vs. undefeated and No. 2–ranked Michigan. It marked the first time in the illustrious series that the teams entered the game ranked No. 1 and 2 in the nation. At stake: the Big Ten championship and a likely spot in the BCS Championship Game.

Thursday night before the game, Bo Schembechler delivered his annual pep talk to the Wolverines. The next morning, the

Quarterback Troy Smith looks to pass against Michigan in Ohio State's 42–39 victory on November 18, 2006. Photo courtesy of Getty Images

77-year-old Hall of Fame coach collapsed and died. The game went on with a then-record crowd of 105,708 at Ohio Stadium. A pregame video tribute to Schembechler was played on the stadium scoreboard as the PA announcer read, "Michigan has lost a coach and patriarch. The Big Ten has lost a legend and icon. Ohio State has lost an alumnus and friend."

Michigan took the opening kickoff and drove 80 yards to take a 7–0 lead. It was their only lead of the game. The Buckeyes scored three unanswered TDs and took a 28–14 advantage into halftime. Midway through the third quarter, Michigan pulled to within 28–24, but Antonio Pittman took the ball for a 56-yard touchdown run to put the Buckeyes ahead 35–24. The Wolverines' Mike Hart scored his third touchdown of the day early in the fourth quarter to cut OSU's lead to 35–31. But, with 5:38 left in the game, the Buckeyes' Brian Robiskie caught a 13-yard TD pass from Troy Smith to make it 42–31. Michigan scored again with 2:16 remaining and converted its two-point try to make it a three-point game at 42–39, but the Buckeyes were able to run out the clock.

Smith threw for 316 yards and four TDs, Ted Ginn Jr. caught eight passes for 104 yards, and Antonio Pittman ran for 139 yards on 18 carries. "There were a lot of good playmakers out there today," said Ohio State coach Jim Tressel. "It was a fast-break game the whole way."

Michigan coach Lloyd Carr said, "We gave up too many big plays. Those are mistakes in a game like this, in any game, that will get you beat."

Ohio State went on to play in the National Championship Game but lost to Florida 41–14. Michigan played Southern Cal in the Rose Bowl and lost 32–18.

No. 2: 1970

MICHIGAN	0	3	6	0	9
OHIO STATE	3	7	0	10	20

In another battle of unbeaten teams, Ohio State was 8–0 and ranked fifth in the nation while Michigan was 9–0 and ranked fourth. That was the year that a judge in Columbus threw out an obscenity charge against a defendant arrested for wearing a T-shirt that read "Fuck Michigan" because the message "accurately expressed" local sentiment about the university and state.

The game began with Michigan fumbling the opening kickoff. Ohio State recovered and quickly went ahead 3–0, but U-M tied the game on the first play of the second quarter. Rex Kern hit Bruce Jankowski for a 26-yard TD to put OSU ahead at halftime 10–3. Michigan scored a touchdown in the third quarter and appeared ready to tie the game, but the Buckeyes' Tim Anderson blocked the PAT kick. Ohio State added a field goal and four-yard TD run by Leo Hayden to win 20–9.

Hayden had 117 yards rushing on 28 carries, while the Buckeyes defense held Michigan to just 37 net rushing yards. OSU linebacker Stan White had a key interception in the fourth quarter.

Following the season, the Buckeyes had four players chosen in the first round of the NFL Draft (John Brockington, Jack Tatum, William Anderson, and Hayden) and 13 players chosen overall.

No. 3: 2002

MICHIGAN	3	6	0	0	9
OHIO STATE	7	0	0	7	14

No. 2 Ohio State (12–0) vs. No. 12 Michigan (9–2) at Ohio Stadium. The Buckeyes' hopes for making it to the national championship game hinged on the final play of the game.

Michigan trailed 14–9 but had the ball at the Ohio State 24-yard line with one second left. "My only thought was, *Who's the guy running the clock?* I mean, one second left? What's that?" said Ohio State linebacker Matt Wilhelm.

Michigan quarterback John Navarre was on his way to setting a school record for passing yards in a season. He threw to Braylon Edwards, a future Big Ten Offensive Player of the Year, at the goal line. But Will Allen, Ohio State's junior nickel back, stepped in front of Edwards and intercepted the pass on the final play of the regular season. "We worked so hard for this," said Allen. "We're 13–0, and you can't beat that."

Michigan had gone ahead 3–0 midway through the opening period, but Ohio State took the lead on a two-yard TD run by Maurice Clarett. Michigan added two second-quarter field goals to take make it 9–7 at halftime. With the score still the same, the Buckeyes took over at their own 37 with 8:40 remaining. Craig Krenzel completed a pass to fullback Brandon Schnittker, then converted a fourth-and-1 with a QB sneak at the Wolverines' 34. Krenzel hit Clarett with a pass to the Michigan 7. Two plays later, Maurice Hall took a pitch and ran it around the right side for a three-yard touchdown.

Michigan didn't quit. The Wolverines drove into OSU territory before Darrion Scott hit Navarre and forced him to fumble. The Buckeyes' Will Smith recovered. But the Buckeyes were unable to run out the clock and gave the ball back to Michigan at the Wolverines' 20-yard line with 56 seconds left. Navarre moved U-M to the OSU 24 before throwing an incompletion in the end zone and the final pass that was intercepted by Allen.

"We knew it was going to be a slugfest. Anyone who thought it was going to be anything other than a game decided at the end hasn't been around the Ohio State–Michigan game," said Ohio State coach Jim Tressel.

The victory put the Buckeyes into the BCS Championship Game at the Fiesta Bowl, where they defeated No. 1 Miami (Florida) for the national championship.

No. 4: 1974

MICHIGAN	10	0	0	0	**10**
OHIO STATE	0	9	3	0	**12**

The Wolverines came into Ohio Stadium with a 10–0 record and No. 3 national ranking. The Buckeyes were 9–1 and ranked No. 4. Ohio State had the Heisman Trophy winner in Archie Griffin and three players chosen in the first round of the NFL Draft. Michigan had an All-American (DB Dave Brown) and seven All–Big Ten players. But the game came down to two relatively unknown kickers.

Ohio State's walk-on kicker, Tom Klaban, a Czechoslovakian refugee, made four field goals, while Michigan's kicker, Mike Lantry (who had missed two field goals late in the 1973 game that ended in a tie) missed a 33-yard field-goal attempt with 18 seconds remaining that would have won the game.

Griffin rushed for 111 yards, while Bruce Elia had a key interception. Klaban's field goals came from 47, 25, 43, and 45 yards.

TOP 5 RUSHING GAMES vs. MICHIGAN

1. **Chris Wells** | 222 yards | 2007
   39 carries, 2 TDs | 14–3 (OSU)

2. **Dave Francis** | 186 yards | 1962
   31 carries, 2 TDs | 28–0 (OSU)

3. **Dan "Boom" Herron** | 175 yards | 2010
   22 carries, TD | 37–7 (OSU)

4. **Carlos Snow** | 170 yards | 1988
   25 carries, TD | 34–31 (U-M)

5t. **Archie Griffin** | 163 yards | 1973
   30 carries | 10–10 (tie)

   Loren "Bob" White | 163 yards | 1957
   30 carries | 31–14 (OSU)

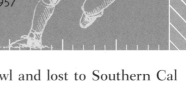

Ohio State went to the Rose Bowl and lost to Southern Cal 18–17, finishing third in the final poll.

No. 5: 1979

OHIO STATE	0	6	6	6	**18**
MICHIGAN	0	7	8	0	**15**

The Buckeyes' Jim Laughlin blocked a Michigan punt, and Todd Bell picked it up and ran it in for a touchdown to give Ohio State an undefeated regular season in Earle Bruce's first year as head coach.

Michigan (8–2 entering the game) started a freshman quarterback—Rich Hewlett—who had taken just four snaps all year. The Buckeyes' defense held the Wolverines in check all day, and Hewlett eventually exited the game with an injury. Art Schlichter threw for 196 yards on just 12 completions, and Jim Gayle had 72 rushing yards on just nine carries.

But it was the postgame riots that contributed to make this game memorable. Even though the game was in Ann Arbor, the Buckeyes faithful were in a mood to celebrate. The first casualty was a car with "Go Michigan" painted on it. The auto was flipped over and set on fire. Soon the police, in full riot gear, approached the revelers. Glass, firecrackers, and cherry bombs were thrown. The police reportedly responded with clubs to disperse the crowd.

The final tally: a school-record 338 arrests.

The final result: the Buckeyes (with future USC coach Pete Carroll on their staff) went to the Rose Bowl and lost to the Trojans 17–16. The defeat dropped the Buckeyes to No. 4 in the final polls.

No. 6: 1934

MICHIGAN	0	0	0	0	0
OHIO STATE	6	6	0	22	34

In the first 30 games of the OSU–U-M series, the Wolverines held a 22–6–2 advantage. Enter Francis A. Schmidt as the new head coach of the Buckeyes. According to legend, here's Schmidt's initial talk to the team:

> My name's Schmidt. I'm the new football coach here. This thing is a football. At one time, it was used here at Ohio State to place behind opponents' goal lines, for which Ohio State was credited with six points. I understand that usage has been sort of overlooked here in recent years. That's not funny. That's tragic. For your information, I'm figuring on reviving the old custom. And one more thing. I want you to remember it from now on: we're going to beat Michigan this year. Yes, beat Michigan. Why not? Those guys put their pants on one leg at a time, the same as you do.

The win over Michigan was the first of four consecutive shut-out victories by Schmidt and the Buckeyes. It also began the tradition of the Gold Pants, awarded to the Ohio State players after a win over Michigan. The Ohio Pants Club, made up of local business leaders, was formed April 17, 1935.

No. 7: 1972

MICHIGAN	0	3	8	0	**11**
OHIO STATE	0	7	7	0	**14**

Ohio State's defense held previously unbeaten Michigan out of the end zone on two fourth-and-goal plays from inside the 1-yard line, while freshman running back Archie Griffin scored what turned out to be the winning touchdown.

The second of the two goal-line stands took place with nine minutes remaining. U-M coach Bo Schembechler eschewed the potentially game-tying field goal and ordered QB Dennis Franklin to attempt a sneak. The OSU defensive line buried him, and the Buckeyes held on for the win.

Ohio State quarterback Greg Hare attempted just three passes all day (one completion, one incompletion, and one interception—perfectly demonstrating Coach Hayes' dictum that, when you pass, three things can happen, and two of them are bad).

The victory put the Buckeyes in the Rose Bowl, where they lost to Southern Cal 42–17. Ohio State finished at No. 9 in the final poll.

No. 8: 1975

OHIO STATE	7	0	0	14	**21**
MICHIGAN	0	7	0	7	**14**

Woody Hayes' Ohio State team beat Michigan…with the pass? Yep. Archie Griffin was held to 46 yards rushing, snapping a streak of 31 consecutive games of 100-plus yards. But QB Cornelius Greene went to the air for the Buckeyes and threw for only 84 yards.

The Buckeyes entered the game at Ann Arbor with a 10–0 record and No. 1 national ranking. Michigan was 8–0–2 and fourth in the polls. Ohio State trailed 14–7 in the final quarter. Pete Johnson tied the score on a plunge with 3:18 to play. It was then that another Griffin—Ray—intercepted Rick Leach's pass and returned it to the Michigan 3-yard line. Johnson scored again to give the Buckeyes the win.

Michigan outgained the Buckeyes 361 yards to 208, but the Wolverines committed five turnovers. "It was the greatest game I ever coached," Hayes said later.

WOODY HAYES ON THE GAME

"How did our great rivalry get started? Well, the real fight started back in 1836 when Andrew Jackson, that wily old cuss, took Toledo away from that state up north and gave it to us."

"I didn't like that SOB when he played for me, I didn't like him when he worked for me, and I certainly don't like him now." (On Schembechler)

"They couldn't beat me with two Michigan coaches. So they had to come down here and take a coach that I trained. And they haven't beaten me with him yet."

"We don't give a damn for the whole state of Michigan."

"Spoiled, hell! I think the bastards are probably trying to poison us or something! Cancel the dinner here tonight. We're making other plans." (When an assistant coach said that the salad smelled funny at a team lunch in Michigan)

"Men, this is war! I don't care anything about the national championship or the Big Ten championship, but if we win this game today and afterward, if the Good Lord says, 'Woody, it's your time,' I'll say, 'Lord, I'm ready!' I'll have to take it easy up there—or down there—but I know where I'll go." (Before the 1975 Michigan game)

"Because I couldn't go for three." (When asked why he went for two in the 1968 Michigan game with a 50–14 lead)

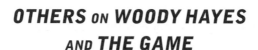

OTHERS ON WOODY HAYES AND THE GAME

"There was something about the Michigan game. Woody could create so much hate between Michigan and Ohio."

—Jim Parker

"Michigan games, he'd have guys crying like they just lost their best friend before they went out on the field."

—Pete Johnson

"I'll buy all the sideline markers Woody Hayes wants to tear up. Ohio State without Hayes would draw at least 30,000 fewer people."

—Michigan AD Don Canham

"In Hayes' view, Ohio boys who enroll at Michigan, especially football players, are either traitors or degenerates, or both. Sometimes it's hard to tell if he's kidding when he talks about Michigan. The consensus is that he isn't."

—Robert Vare

The fans in Columbus were overjoyed and took to the streets. To disperse the crowd, police fired "knee-knockers" (one-inch wooden projectiles) at the rioters. Forty-eight people were arrested. Ah, the magical '70s.

No. 9: 1954

MICHIGAN	7	0	0	0	7
OHIO STATE	0	7	0	14	21

This win gave Woody Hayes his first Big Ten title, first trip to the Rose Bowl, and first undefeated regular season. The game was tied 7–7 at halftime, and Michigan drove to within a foot of the goal line in the third quarter. But Buckeyes lineman Jim Parker stopped the Wolverines' Dave Hill, and the tide turned. Ohio State drove 99 yards for the go-ahead score, a Dave Leggett–to–Dick Brubaker pass. Following an interception by Howard "Hopalong" Cassady, the Buckeyes added an insurance TD on Cassady's one-yard run.

Hayes got everyone's attention in the locker room after the game. "There's just one thing I want to say!" he shouted. He got up on a table, jumped off, and yelled, "Whoopee!"

In the Rose Bowl, the Buckeyes beat Southern Cal 20–7 to complete the 10–0 season. Ohio State was voted No. 1 in the nation in the Associated Press poll following the game.

No. 10: 1987

OHIO STATE	0	7	13	3	23
MICHIGAN	7	6	7	0	20

After nine seasons, an 80–26–1 overall record, a 56–17 Big Ten won-loss mark, four Big Ten titles, and a 5–3 record in bowl games, Earle Bruce was told that he was going to be the coach of the Ohio State Buckeyes for just five more days.

That was Monday. The OSU–U-M game was Saturday. The 5–4–1 Buckeyes were facing a 7–3 Michigan team in Ann Arbor. Bruce entered the game with a 4–4 lifetime record against the Wolverines. Bruce said, "I guess they've got a right to fire a guy. I think it's very poor timing, though, right before the Michigan game." Bruce told his team, "I have been let go by the university. This is the most important game in your entire life. The school up north is good, but they're not great. Strap on your helmets, boys, because there is no game like this one, and we'll be flying around the field and cracking heads. This will be the hardest-hitting game of your lives. We are going to go up to Michigan, and we are going to kick their ass."

The Buckeyes players wore headbands with EARLE on them. But the Wolverines jumped to a 13–0 lead. Just before halftime, Ohio State got on the scoreboard. Linebacker Mike McCray recovered a Michigan fumble, and Tom Tupa connected with Everett Ross for a four-yard touchdown pass. Said Buckeyes linebacker Chris Spielman, "We didn't make a lot of adjustments at halftime. We didn't have to. Someone mentioned that we had 30 minutes of our football season remaining. No one needed to say anything more."

On their first possession of the third quarter, the Buckeyes scored on a 70-yard touchdown pass from Tupa to Carlos Snow to take a 14–13 lead. Later in the quarter, Tupa scored on a one-yard sneak, but the extra point kick was no good, leaving Ohio State with a 20–13 advantage. Before the third period ended, Michigan tied the game on a 10-yard run by Leroy Hoard.

Howard "Hopalong" Cassady leaps between Michigan defenders to score the final TD in Ohio State's 21–7 victory on November 20, 1954, giving Woody Hayes his first Big Ten title on the way to a national championship.

OSU's defense stiffened, and Matt Frantz booted a 26-yard field goal for the winning points with 5:18 remaining. When the game ended, the Buckeyes carried Bruce around the field.

Afterward, Spielman said, "They [the OSU administration] shouldn't have fired Coach Bruce when they did or the way they did, and we players came back and won the football game because none of us thought it was right."

No. 11: 2005

OHIO STATE	6	6	0	13	**25**
MICHIGAN	0	7	11	3	**21**

Buckeyes quarterback Troy Smith led a comeback in the final minutes, giving the Buckeyes a share of the Big Ten championship.

Michigan led 21–12 midway through the fourth quarter when Smith and the offense caught fire. First, it was Smith connecting with Santonio Holmes on a 26-yard TD pass that pulled the Buckeyes to within 21–19 with 6:40 to go. Michigan drove to the OSU 34-yard line and opted for a pooch punt instead of trying a field goal.

The Buckeyes and Smith took over on the Ohio State 12-yard line with 4:16 remaining. Here's how it happened: Troy Smith passes to Ted Ginn Jr. for nine yards; Antonio Pittman runs for two. First down on the OSU 23. Smith throws an incomplete pass, then on second down completes to Ginn for 11 yards. First down on the OSU 34. Smith passes to Ginn for

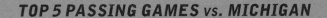

TOP 5 PASSING GAMES vs. MICHIGAN

1. **Joe Germaine** | 330 yards | 1998
   16-for-28, 3 TDs | 31–16 (OSU)

2. **Troy Smith** | 316 yards | 2006
   29-for-41, 4 TDs | 42–39 (OSU)

3. **Troy Smith** | 300 yards | 2005
   27-for-37, TD | 25–21 (OSU)

4. **Mike Tomczak** | 298 yards | 1983
   21-for-40, TD | 24–21 (U-M)

5. **Bobby Hoying** | 286 yards | 1995
   22-for-45, TD | 31–23 (U-M)

OHIO STATE

six yards, then throws to Holmes for seven. First down on the OSU 47. Smith passes to Holmes for 11 yards. First down on the U-M 42. Smith runs for five yards, then passes to Holmes for six. First down on the U-M 31. Timeout OSU with 0:47 remaining. Time resumes, and Smith completes a 27-yard pass to Anthony Gonzalez. First down on the U-M 4. Timeout with 0:37 left. Out of the break, Smith runs and is stopped for no gain. Timeout at 0:29. Second down, Pittman runs it in from four yards out and the touchdown.

The drive covered 88 yards in 12 plays and took 3:54. Final score: Ohio State 25, Michigan 21. Smith completed 27 of 37 passes for a career high 300 yards and one TD.

OHIO STATE

TOP 5 TIES *IN* THE GAME

1. 1973 (10–10). The Buckeyes entered the game at Ann Arbor with a 9–0 record and ranked No. 1 in the nation. The Wolverines entered at 10–0 and ranked No. 4. OSU built a 10–0 halftime lead but went for it on fourth-and-2 at the Michigan 34 in the third quarter. The Wolverines stopped the Buckeyes and got a quick field goal to cut it to 10–3. With 9:32 remaining, Michigan tied the game when QB Dennis Franklin ran it in on a fourth-and-1 play from OSU's 10. Ohio State got the Rose Bowl berth despite Bo's whining and beat Southern Cal 42–21. The Buckeyes finished No. 2 in the final poll (behind Notre Dame), and U-M wound up No. 6 (no bowl for poor Bo).

2. 1949 (7–7). Both teams had 4–1 conference records. The Wolverines were favored by seven points at home and went ahead 7–0 in the first quarter, scoring on a short pass play after the Buckeyes' punter fumbled a snap. The Buckeyes tied things in the fourth quarter on a short run by Fred Morrison. The tie sent Ohio State to the Rose Bowl, where the Buckeyes beat Cal 17–14.

3. 1992 (13–13). Ohio State coach John Cooper, 0–4 against U-M to that point, was accused of playing for a tie in order to avoid losing to the Wolverines again. The Buckeyes, playing at home, scored a TD with 4:24 to play to pull to within 13–12. Cooper ordered the Buckeyes to kick the extra point,

continues

rather than go for two. "With over four minutes to play, [a two-point conversion] never crossed my mind. The idea was to hold them, get the ball back, and kick a winning field goal," Cooper said. OSU did get the ball back but elected to punt on fourth-and-4 on the Michigan 49-yard line with 1:28 remaining. Following the game, OSU president Gordon Gee said the tie with the 8–0–3 Wolverines was "one of our greatest wins." Well, no. But it was one of our greatest ties.

4. 1941 (20–20). In his first season as the Ohio State coach, Paul Brown led the Buckeyes to a tie with the heavily favored Wolverines in Ann Arbor. Both teams entered the game with 6–1 records. The Buckeyes led 7–0. Michigan led 14–7. The Buckeyes tied it at 14, then took the lead with 12 minutes remaining on a long pass from Jack Graf to Dick Fisher, but missed the extra-point kick. Michigan scored on the ensuing possession, tying the score on a five-yard run by Robert Westfall, but also missed its extra point. Neither team threatened to score again in the final 6:00, and neither team played in a bowl game. Minnesota went 8–0 and was voted the national champion.

5. 1900 (0–0). In the first 11 games of the series, Michigan outscored Ohio State 319–18, compiling a 10–0–1 record. The lone tie came in the second game of the series, in Ann Arbor. Ohio State had 136 yards of offense and held the vaunted Michigan attack to just 74 yards. Ohio State finished the season at 8–1–1; Michigan was 7–2–1.

OHIO STATE

TOP 5 RECEIVING GAMES VS. MICHIGAN

1. **David Boston** | 217 yards | 1998
   10 catches, 2 TDs | 31–16 (OSU)

2. **Michael Jenkins** | 132 yards | 2003
   9 catches | 35–21 (U-M)

3. **John Frank** | 123 yards | 1983
   10 catches | 24–21 (U-M)

4. **Santonio Holmes** 121 yards | 2003
   8 catches, 2 TDs | 35–21 (U-M)

5. **Brian Stablein** | 111 yards | 1992
   12 catches | 13–13 (tie)

"There will be a lot of No. 10 jerseys and a lot of kids on Thanksgiving weekend trying to make those moves in a pile of leaves," said Buckeyes coach Jim Tressel.

No. 12: 1968

MICHIGAN	7	7	0	0	**14**
OHIO STATE	7	14	6	23	**50**

The Buckeyes were 9–0, Michigan 8–1. Ohio State had a young squad, the Wolverines had a veteran team. But that day in Ohio Stadium, the Buckeyes surprised everyone, including themselves.

Ohio State dominated Michigan on both sides of the ball. OSU outgained the Wolverines 567 yards to 311. Fullback Jim Otis led the way for the Buckeyes with four touchdowns and 143 rushing yards. Quarterback Rex Kern ran for two TDs, completed 5 of 8 passes for 41 yards, and rushed for another 96 yards.

The game was not without controversy. Following the Buckeyes' final touchdown with three minutes remaining, Woody Hayes called for the Buckeyes to go for a two-point conversion. Why? Maybe it was to try to match OSU's largest margin of victory in the series (38 points in the 1935 game). Whatever the reason, after the game, Hayes was asked why. "Because I couldn't go for three," he said.

It was the final game at Michigan for Wolverines coach Bump Elliott. The Buckeyes went to the Rose Bowl and came from behind to beat Southern Cal 27–16. Ohio State topped the final AP and Coaches' national polls.

No. 13: 1981

OHIO STATE	0	7	0	7	**14**
MICHIGAN	3	0	6	0	**9**

The Ohio State win was one of the brightest days in the up-and-down career of Art Schlichter. The underdog Buckeyes (Michigan began the season ranked No. 1 in the nation but were 8–2 entering the game) trailed 3–0 in the second quarter at the always sold-out Michigan Stadium. But Schlichter mixed passes with runs by Tim Spencer to move the Buckeyes 82 yards and within a foot of the goal line. Schlichter

Buckeyes quarterback Art Schlichter (10) is lifted into the air by receiver Gary Williams after scoring a second-quarter touchdown in Ohio State's 14–9 victory over Michigan on November 21, 1981, in Ann Arbor.

snuck it in from there to give Ohio State a 7–3 halftime advantage.

Michigan responded with two third-quarter field goals to retake the lead, 9–7. Michigan was driving again when Kevin Bell intercepted a pass in the end zone. Schlichter then led the Buckeyes 80 yards for the game-winner. The QB scrambled into the end zone from six yards out with less than three minutes remaining.

Schlichter completed 12 of 24 passes for 131 yards and was carried off the field on the shoulders of his teammates. Spencer rushed for 110 yards on 25 carries. But the Buckeyes defense came up big, too. It kept Michigan out of the end zone, despite the Wolverines moving inside the 10-yard line four times. The Buckeyes intercepted three passes and recovered one fumble.

Said Schembechler: "We shouldn't have lost. This is one game we should have won. We simply squandered too many opportunities. I didn't expect to lose. They only had two drives on us. Other than that, they didn't do anything."

The win gave the Buckeyes a share of the Big Ten title at 6–2. Ohio State beat Navy in the Liberty Bowl 31–28 to finish 9–3 and No. 12 in the final Coaches' poll.

No. 14: 2004

MICHIGAN	14	0	0	7	**21**
OHIO STATE	7	13	14	3	**37**

On paper, it looked like a mismatch. Both teams began the season ranked among the nation's top 10. But 10 weeks later, Michigan was 7–0 in the Big Ten, and the Buckeyes were 3–4.

Sophomore Troy Smith began the season as the backup quarterback. But the starter, Justin Zwick, was injured midway through the season. Enter Smith. The Buckeyes would win four of the five games with Smith at QB, but he saved his breakout game for the biggest stage: Michigan at Ohio Stadium.

Smith played error-free football, running for 145 yards and one touchdown on 18 carries and throwing for 241 yards and two touchdowns. He became the first Buckeyes player to run for more than 100 yards and throw for more than 200 in a game. Smith (who wasn't sacked all day) also directed the Buckeyes on scoring drives of 99 and 97 yards.

The Buckeyes rolled up 446 yards of total offense on just 70 plays and outscored Michigan 27–0 in the second and third quarters. In addition, freshman Ted Ginn Jr. returned a punt 82 yards for a touchdown. It was his fourth punt return for a TD that season, setting Ohio State and Big Ten records and tying the NCAA mark.

Smith summed up his day: "I didn't realize what this rivalry was about and is about until you get a W, until you're in it, until you're in the fight. My hat's off to Michigan, but today was Ohio State's day."

The loss didn't prevent Michigan from playing in the Rose Bowl (which they lost to Texas). But the win did put Ohio State in the Alamo Bowl, where the Buckeyes beat Les Miles' Oklahoma State team 33–7.

No. 15: 1944

MICHIGAN	0	7	0	7	14
OHIO STATE	6	0	6	6	18

Les Horvath, granted a fourth year of eligibility while he was attending dental school at Ohio State, made the most of his extra season, winning the Heisman Trophy and leading the Buckeyes to a 9–0 record and top spot in the national polls.

Yet the perfect season hung in the balance in the season finale versus Michigan (8–1 entering the game). The Buckeyes trailed 7–6 at halftime, but Horvath took advantage of a Michigan fumble to score from a yard out, giving Ohio State a 12 7 advantage. Michigan regained the lead, 14–12, with 8:29 remaining.

After Michigan's onside kick attempt went out of bounds, the Buckeyes drove 52 yards for the winning TD. Horvath dove in from the 1 with 3:16 left. Richard Flanagan sealed the win with an interception in the final minute.

Horvath was the offensive hero, but Buckeyes All-America lineman Bill Hackett caused two fumbles, both recovered by OSU captain Gordon Appleby.

2

WE LOVE BEATING EVERYONE

HOW COULD WE TOP THIS LIST of the top 10 non-series Buckeyes victories with anything other than the 2003 Fiesta Bowl and the resulting *national championship* victory against Miami? Easy. Do you remember the 1984 home game against Illinois? It was between that one—we labored most of a night over this—and Appalachian State's victory over Michigan in 2007. Okay, a cheap shot...but we got it in, so we win.

No. 1: October 13, 1984 vs. Illinois

ILLINOIS	17	7	11	3	38
OHIO STATE	0	21	14	10	45

No one really was certain how well Ohio State would bounce back from a defeat at Purdue the previous week. By the time 13 seconds of the second quarter had elapsed in Ohio Stadium against Illinois, almost every soul in the the Horseshoe was completely certain. The Buckeyes, as if hit by a stun gun, trailed 24–0. The lights that were illuminating the field suddenly became brighter, the focus a lot more intense, and the boos—*boos?*—as loud as anyone could recall at that time. (Of course, this was before Jim Colletto called for Greg Frey, not exactly known for his rushing proficiency, to run a naked bootleg to the strong side of the field on fourth-and-1 in the waning minutes against Michigan to "save" the game during another season. He lost yardage. Michigan won. Shit!) We were sitting up against the press box in C Deck, bemoaning every friggin' play that was a bust, and it seemed, in the beginning, each one certainly was that, if less. Here's how it unfolded:

First Quarter—Illinois drove 80 yards in 11 plays after an OSU punt. Illini quarterback Jack Trudeau drilled a three-yard pass to Randy Grant for the first touchdown. After another Buckeyes punt, Illinois set up shop at its own 34, and Trudeau passed them into position for Chris White's 26-yard field goal. By this point, the natives were getting restless. Smuggled-in flasks began to appear.... Buckeyes quarterback Mike Tomczak was intercepted on the next Ohio State play, and from the OSU 21, the Illini began a short scoring march that was culminated by Trudeau's 10-yard touchdown pass to David Williams. Score? 17–0. Commence the venomous cursing, the kind with spittle flying in all directions. Certainly, Coach Earle Bruce had some kind of antidote up his sleeve. Maybe?

Second Quarter—Well, no. Not yet, at least. On OSU's first play after the kickoff, tailback Keith Byars fumbled the ball. The Illini had the ball at the Ohio State 21, and the drooling among the Orange and Blue was palpable. Let the trash-talking begin. There was lots of woofing from the other side, a lot of nodding, posturing, fingers pointing to the scoreboard. It made a youngish man want to bound out of the upper reaches of the stadium, go down to the field, and deliver a haymaker to anyone from Illinois in his way. The problem was, that would be against the law, and he would be tossed from the stadium and sent to the can. Not a terrific idea. Okay, then, Illinois scored quickly, Trudeau passing to Cap Boso for eight yards. Uh, 24–0. (Should we just take off for the Varsity Club now? Sonofabitch!)... After an Illinois punt pinned the Buckeyes at their own 9, the slumbering bunch awakened. Tomczak hit Cris Carter for 36 and 17 yards, and Byars found the end zone on a 16-yard run. Huh, maybe we have something here. 24–7.... We *do!* Rich Spangler's onside kick was bungled badly by Illinois, and Joe Jenkins pounced on it for the Buckeyes. We now had the ball at their 31. Byars gained a yard, and then T-czak hit Carter with a 33-yard strike. The bitching had ceased. 24–14, just a little less than three and a half minutes before halftime. The Illini stayed with the pass, and one of Trudeau's was intercepted by Sonny Gordon, giving OSU the ball at its 38. T-czak passed 19 yards to Carter, nine yards to Doug Smith twice, and nine yards to Mike Lanese once. From there, Byars took it in from the 4, making a dive across the goal line at the last instant. What do you know? 24–21. Halftime. The place was buzzing. Everyone wanted halftime to last about as long as a timeout.

Third Quarter—OSU kicked off, and the Illini fumbled. Are you kidding? Terry White recovered at the Illinois 26. Seriously! Byars covered all the yardage in four plays, and—*whoa!* Zippity doo-dah, kiddo. Bing. Bang. *Boom!* 28-24! On the next series, Illinois drove 41 yards to the Ohio State 29, from where White lifted a 46-yarder through the uprights. Uh-Oh! 28–27. Following the kickoff, Byars banged his way for 15 yards, the Buckeyes had a stupid movement penalty, and then Byars blasted through the line for a 67-yard TD run! (More about that later.) Here we go, Buckeyes, here we go! 35–27....

TOP 5 OSU RUSHING GAMES OF ALL-TIME

1. **Eddie George** | 314 yards | 1995
   36 carries, 3 TDs | 41–3 vs. Illinois (W)

2. **Keith Byars** | 274 yards | 1984
   39 carries, 5 TDs | 45–38 vs. Illinois (W)

3. **Archie Griffin** | 246 yards | 1973
   30 carries, TD | 55–13 vs. Iowa (W)

4. **Archie Griffin** | 239 yards | 1972
   27 carries, TD | 29–14 vs. North Carolina (W)

5. **Raymont Harris** | 235 yards | 1993
   39 carries, 3 TDs | 28–21 vs. BYU (W, Holiday Bowl)

OHIO STATE

The Buckeyes were later forced to punt, and Trudeau directed the Illini on a 10-play, 63-yard scoring drive, capped by his pass to Wilson. Then he added a two-point conversion by running it in. Crap! 35-all.

Fourth Quarter—After Illinois kicked off, T-czak had the Buckeyes back in motion, but the drive, which featured a 17-yard completion to Carter, stalled at the Illini 30. Here comes Spangler, and he drills a 46-yard field goal. A little breathing room, 38–35. Those clock-eating Illini. They took possession on the next series at their own 22 and methodically tramped up the field on a 17-play (*seventeen!*) drive. The defense *had* to be gassed by this point. Not true. The OSU defenders figuratively punched Illinois in the throat, stopping Thomas Rooks on a run from one yard outside the end zone. In comes White, though, and he connected on a 16-yard field goal that was more difficult (the angles are tough) than one would think. Pass the flask, please. 38-all. (In truth, we wished these guys would have played forever. What one team took, the other took back. Classic!) Ohio State settled for a touchback on the ensuing kickoff and set up shop at its own 20. Byars ripped off 23 yards on the first play, and the 'Shoe was rockin'! There would be nine more rushes on the 11-play drive (right down their friggin' throats!), the last of which was a Byars run in from the 3 with 36 measly seconds left. Oh, yeah! *Hell* yeah! Let's just stand here and soak it all in. Screw dinner reservations. This is one to remember! 45–38.

Oh, and that 67-yard scoring run by Byars, the one that put Ohio State ahead 35–27? Yeah, it was a thing of beauty— especially after the Dayton Dominator lost a wheel with 40 yards to go. Well, really it was a shoe, but stay with us here. Byars, unbeknownst to anyone in the crowd—or anywhere else, for that matter—was on his way to a record-setting day. That, in the wake of being physically battered the week before at Purdue. He eclipsed Archie Griffin's standard of 246 yards against Iowa (on 30 carries producing one touchdown) with a Herculean effort that totaled 274 yards on 39 carries. He also tied Pete Johnson's school record with five touchdowns in this game. About his clinching touchdown run, he told Tim May of the *Columbus Dispatch*, "I just had to suck it up and go. I put my ears back and said, 'You've got to go get it. Stop me.'" They couldn't. Said Bruce, "This is the greatest comeback I've ever been associated with." No arguments, Coach.

No. 2: January 3, 2003, Fiesta Bowl (2OT)

OHIO STATE	0	14	3	0	7	7	**31**
MIAMI (FLA.)	7	0	7	3	7	0	**24**

Not since 1968—well, January 1, 1969, to be technical—had one play so thoroughly defined a title team for Ohio State. We know what you're thinking. We know you're saluting Matt Wilhelm for knocking down what would have proved to be a disastrous touchdown for Miami in the second overtime of the Buckeyes' 31–24 victory. In truth, the game was won earlier on that last-gasp play when Buckeyes undersized linebacker Cie Grant, knowing everything was on the line and more determined than ever, muscled his way into the pocket to pressure Hurricanes quarterback Ken Dorsey into a pass that was completely off the mark, leaving Wilhelm alone to end the threat. It's almost as if Wilhelm were alone at the plate during batting practice. Dorsey served up something of a softball. *Swat!* Game, set, and match. If this were a basketball game, Grant would get the assist. And with that one play, the scarlet-clad sea of Buckeye Nation in Sun Devil Stadium went berserk. Tostitos for everyone! The finest hour had been attained once more. Can it get more exciting than that? Ever? Doubt it. Sure, we'll give props to Auburn for its January 10, 2011, BCS National Championship–winning, 22–19 victory against Oregon as time expired, but it wasn't close to OSU's vanquishing of Miami in terms of sheer drama.

A definite underdog entering the game, the Buckeyes turned No. 1 Miami and its high-powered offense away time and again, while clawing its way for every yard it earned on offense and denied to Miami on defense.

Jim Tressel, who had won four national titles in Division I-AA, stood before an international television audience and those in the stadium from the deck of a confetti-showered make-shift stage on the field, and said, "We've always had the best damn band in the land, now we've got the best damn *team* in the land."

How can you not love this Ohio State defense? Four stops of the Hurricanes from the Ohio State 2? Twice? Are you kidding us? Miami came in averaging 42 points a game and 475 yards of total offense. The Hurricanes trailed 17–7 and had belched up two of their five turnovers of the game in the first half. And there went the, uh, swagger. Oh, there was a nice little comeback to force the game into overtime, and, yes, the Ohio State offense took a long winter's nap in the second half until quarterback Craig Krenzel got things going again, but OSU faithful had to feel good, *really* good about the Buckeyes' chances in overtime—yes, even after Todd Sievers' 40-yard field goal with 0:00 showing in regulation.

So, no second consecutive championship for the 'Canes, and, uh, so long to a 35th consecutive victory, Miami. We heard Woody Hayes say this once: "It's not enough to succeed. Others must fail." Success and failure on the same night never tasted so good to Ohio State loyalists.

This game had it all, and things looked tenuous—as was the case much of the season during which the Buckeyes won seven games by seven or fewer points—when Miami had a 24–17 edge in the first overtime. But on fourth-and-14, Krenzel rekindled hopes with a 17-yard strike to Michael Jenkins. Many times that season, either the offense or the defense

Ohio State tailback Maurice Clarett (13) breaks through to the end zone against Miami (Fla.) for a touchdown in the second overtime of the 2003 Fiesta Bowl, giving the Buckeyes a 31–24 win and a national championship.

would come to the rescue of the other. Four plays later, looking down the barrels of a tie-it-or-go-home situation, Krenzel threw an incompletion. Miami began celebrating. Wildly. With swagger. However, in the words of Lee Corso, the colorful *ESPN College GameDay* analyst, "Not so fast, my friend." See, there was one miniscule detail that needed

A TOST' AND OFFERING

This is clever. *This* we love. The morning after the Buckeyes won the national title in the desert against Miami, a very wise and creative soul made his way to Union Cemetery in Columbus. Upon reaching Coach Woody Hayes' gravesite, he placed a bag of Tostitos against the gravestone. We view this as a fitting tribute to the man who did so much to keep OSU football at the top and a stroke of genius on the part of the chap to offer a memento of the national championship season to the late coach.

to be addressed: *pass interference!* Sorry, Glenn Sharpe, for bringing *that* up again.

The Buckeyes had destabilized one of the greatest and most volatile offenses in college football. "They didn't stop us," said Miami tight end Kellen Winslow Jr. in the postgame interview room in the bowels of Sun Devil Stadium. "We did ourselves." Uh-huh. As for Heisman Trophy finalist Dorsey? He was sacked three times, threw two interceptions, fumbled once, and was decked several times. Said Miami coach Larry Coker, who had just lost his first game since going to South Florida, "They're very good at what they did. It sort of caused us problems. They have a great defensive football team." No kidding?

After the Ohio State defense buttoned up the title, the massive Buckeyes throng went crazy in Sun Devil. "Our crowd was electric," said Tressel in a press conference the morning after, owing the charge to a huge Arizona-based clan of

OSU alumni. "They energized our kids. That's what a national championship game should look like...double overtime. Two great heavyweights slugging it out." Led, in the end, by their general—Grant.

No. 3: January 1, 1969: Rose Bowl

OHIO STATE	0	10	3	14	27
USC	0	10	0	6	16

Let's be honest here. No. 1 Ohio State really wasn't supposed to beat the University of Southern California (USC, or the University of Spoiled Children) in the Granddaddy of Them All. There had been about 40-some days of inactivity since the Buckeyes, loaded across the board with talented sophomores, pasted Michigan 50–14 in the regular season finale. Coach Woody Hayes was worried. Too much sun. Too many Hollywood types. Too many distractions. Too much Disneyland. Too much beef at Lawry's. Too much everything, and not nearly enough football—certainly not nearly enough Rex Kern, who missed 10 practices with shoulder issues. Oh, and one more thing: too much O.J. Simpson, the Heisman Trophy–winning tailback turned (eventually) convict. Everyone outside the inner circle expected Simpson to run roughshod over the Buckeyes and for USC to simply cruise to a national championship.

But, as the old saw goes, that is precisely why they play the game. And so, after the Trojans took a 3–0 lead—after a shockingly scoreless first quarter—and the Ohio State offense sputtered, No. 2 USC got the ball on its own 20-yard line. Simpson, perhaps in a precursor to his future Hertz Rent-a-Car commercials, took a deep pitch to the left, and he zigged,

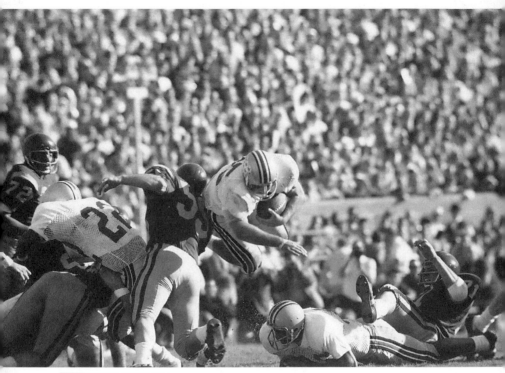

Fullback Jim Otis, Ohio State's leading rusher in the 1969 Rose Bowl versus USC, dives for extra yardage to the Trojans 25-yard line during the 27–16 upset victory that capped the Buckeyes' national championship season.

zagged, shimmied, leapt, spun, and then flat-out out-sprinted, with an escort of blockers, Ohio State defenders the rest of the 80 yards to paydirt. As much as we hate to admit it, Simpson's run was a thing of beauty and nothing experienced by the Buckeyes all season long. Were they shaken? We'd find out, but wasn't this the same bunch that derailed the Heisman candidacy of Purdue's all-everything running back, Leroy Keyes, earlier in the season, shocking the then No. 1–ranked Boilermakers 13–0 in Columbus? (Answer: hell yes.) Hayes later said—and diagrammed how in his own book, *Hotline to*

Victory—that Simpson could have run the ball all the way to the Pacific Ocean on that play. Our estimation: he actually could have made it to Guam, which is not the end of the world, but you can see it from there.

And so the Trojans, all pumped up about their 10–0 lead, had every reason to be concerned, when they, having failed to drive for a potential 17–0 lead, found themselves staring down the barrels of a 10-point, eight-minute rebound by the Buckeyes. First, Kern, the eventual Player of the Game, directed a masterful 13-play, 69-yard drive, capped by a one-yard plunge by fullback Jim Otis. Then, as the clock got perilously close to expiring, Jim Roman nailed a field goal of 26 yards: 10-all at the half. Maybe this wouldn't be the Simpson Show after all.

In the second half, the OSU defense turned up the heat, treating USC quarterback Steve Sogge like a rag doll, and the Buckeyes defenders mostly bottled up Simpson (who totaled 171 yards on the ground, including those 80 from his magnificent run), recovered three fumbles, and intercepted two passes, allowing the offense to become superlative once more. Halfback Leo Hayden churned out 90 yards, and Kern added 35 on the ground while throwing for 101. It was Hayes at his best in the second half, proving three yards and a cloud of dust would win this day. To be truthful, to USC it was 3.98 yards and a cloud of "What the hell was *that*?" nearly every time the Buckeyes touched the ball, although Kern did have touchdown passes of four yards to Hayden and 16 yards to Ray Gillian. In the end, the Buckeyes prevailed 27–16 in Pasadena and became national champions. (Quick! Someone grab a case of Gambrinus!)

After the game, the horde of media wanted to know from Hayes whether this was his greatest team. "Well, it won its ninth game [the laugher against Michigan] more decisively," Woody told sports editor Paul Hornung of the *Columbus Dispatch*. "But, hell, I knew we'd win when we were behind 10–0. We have a good team."

Otis, perhaps, had the best summary. He told the *Dispatch*, "In a game like this, a game between two great teams, you can win it or lose it 20 times. It's life and death on 20 different plays. I said in the huddle, 'Simpson's run is just one play. Now let's just do our regular stuff.'" And that was more than enough on this day.

No. 4: January 1, 1974: Rose Bowl

OHIO STATE	7	7	13	15	42
USC	3	11	7	0	21

Sweet revenge? You bet! One year after Ohio State was embarrassed 42–17 by Southern Cal in the 59th playing of the Rose Bowl, the Buckeyes had roared through the season with a purpose. Everyone expected the Trojans to be back in this game. Ohio State? Well, the questions surfaced about how this team would bounce back after the Pasadena shellacking, and the season hadn't gone exactly as planned. There was, after all, that 10–10 sister-kisser against the school up north. Oh, Michigan could have been USC's opponent had six of the Big Ten athletics directors not voted Ohio State into the game after the teams tied for the conference championship. Aw, too bad.

Still, the way Ohio State played this day, a legitimate claim to No. 1 could be made. Alas, the media and coaches voted Notre Dame the national champion. No matter, though, for this game meant everything to the Buckeyes, who, for 364 days, were tormented by the fact that they just flat fell apart against USC the previous year.

Dick Otte of the *Columbus Dispatch* quoted Coach Woody Hayes as saying, "The greatest victory I ever had…and it may be the greatest victory *we* ever had." Was this, then, the best team you ever had, Coach? "We had some that didn't lose any, but didn't tie, either. It's difficult to say…. They were the greatest team today. We have never been this good in the Rose Bowl."

USC's coach, John McKay, though, didn't mince words in his postgame analysis of what had just happened: "They're the best football team we played this year [perhaps a shot at rival Notre Dame]. They were the much better team today. Give them the credit. We just weren't good enough. Ohio State played better and won." Perhaps an assist for this one should be credited to Hayes' old friend, Ara Parseghian, the Notre Dame coach, who told Hayes the Buckeyes would have to control the ball against the Trojans. Parseghian's Fighting Irish earlier that season had beaten USC 23–14 at South Bend.

Control the ball they did. But they churned out 20 first downs in a highly uncustomary way for Ohio State—they *passed* for six of them! Yes, quarterback Cornelius Greene actually was unleashed to pass the ball. As a matter of fact, the Buckeyes worked on the passing game in each of 15 pre–Rose Bowl practices. He threw eight times, completing six for 129 unexpected yards. And Woody stuck to the game plan even after Greene was intercepted on the third play of the game. At that time, everyone watching or listening the world over probably expected the coach to revert to his cherished running attack. But no, he stayed the course. And Greene actually was known as a running quarterback, folks, one of the three backfield monsters the Buckeyes would feature all season long with Heisman Trophy winner Archie Griffin at tailback and bruising fullback Pete Johnson joining their signal-caller. For the game, the offense averaged 5.47 yards rushing the ball and an unheard-of (for Ohio State, that is) 21.5 yards passing it. Fred Pagac, who later would become OSU's popular defensive coordinator of the Silver Bullets under coach John Cooper, caught four of the six passes for 89 yards. Wingback Brian Baschnagel pulled in one for 25 yards, and David Hazel had the other for a 15-yard gain. This was Ohio State?

Before we get too carried away, it should be pointed out that Griffin shredded the USC defense for 149 yards on 22 carries, including one for a 47-yard, door-slamming touchdown late in the game. Johnson amassed 94 yards on 21 carries and had touchdown runs of one, one, and four yards; while Greene picked up 45 yards on seven carries.

After battling to a 14–14 tie by halftime, the Buckeyes trailed 21–14 after a one-yard run by Anthony Davis. They then rededicated themselves to the memory of the previous year and fairly poured it on for the rest of the second half, which included a stunning 56-yard punt return by Neal Colzie to set up a Greene touchdown run. Said the Miami native, "We had everyone rushing, trying to block the kick. I was

MONK-Y BUSINESS

On the Buckeyes' previous visit to Pasadena in 1973, Coach Woody Hayes had the entire Buckeyes football contingent holed up before the game in a mountainside monastery. No hotel room service. No visits from girlfriends and family. Just...a...lot...of...silence. It's the way the monks live. And it's the way the Buckeyes played the next day in a 42–17 loss to Southern Cal—like monks. So, on this trip, the contingent reverted to the hotel scene, and the players had more freedom, too, with a later curfew and the chance just to be normal after several long days on the practice field. The looseness certainly paid off with a 42–21 defeat of the Trojans,

OHIO STATE

supposed to fair-catch it.... I saw an opening, so I took my chances." He also took one in jubilation, when he spiked the ball out of bounds after his return. The refs saw it and flagged him for unsportsmanlike conduct. Colzie was a wonderfully gifted athlete, one who could probably play any skill position on offense or defense, but for Ohio State he was an All-America defensive back and a punt returner. Once back from the West Coast, one of us asked him what the hell he was thinking when he spiked the ball. He grinned that trademark, wide-angle grin, turned somewhat sheepish, and said, "I guess I wasn't. I was too caught up in the moment...after what they did to us the year before."

They didn't do it this time.

No. 5: October 18, 1975 vs. Wisconsin

WISCONSIN	0	0	0	0	0
OHIO STATE	7	21	14	14	56

We decided to include this one for two reasons: 1) it was as thorough an ass-whupping as that season's team would administer, and 2) because the 2010 Badgers kept Ohio State out of the BCS National Championship game. Take that!

The mid-October day dawned dreary; a lot of clouds and a bit of rain. We told our dear friend, Norton, visiting from Mississauga, Ontario, Canada, for his first OSU game, that it wouldn't be too exciting, that it wouldn't be a score-fest, that the Buckeyes would win but also that it wouldn't be pretty. Never were we happier to be wrong.

Actually, this one was over before it started. Ohio State was ranked No. 1; Wisconsin wasn't ranked at all and, to be fair, was nothing more than an average team at 2–3 but with two losses it shouldn't have had to endure.

This was, as it turned out, a clinic of overpowering, precision football. After fullback Pete Johnson barreled in from a yard out on Ohio State's second possession of the game—capping a 13-play, 92-yard march through and over the Badgers' defense—the rout was on. Wisconsin fumbled and bumbled, if not stumbled, its way through the rest of the game. The OSU defensive pressure was overwhelming (Wisconsin fumbled 10 times and lost five, two of which were recovered by OSU defensive end Pat Curto), and the offensive attack was purely on the money from that first scoring drive on. Cornelius

Greene raced 26 yards after Curto recovered a fumble at the Wisconsin 31, and Johnson blasted through defenders from there, 14–0. Then, after stopping the Badgers on the ensuing possession, Tim Fox fielded a punt at the OSU 25 and wended his way for a 75-yard punt return, after which he introduced the Fox Flip in the end zone. The Ohio Stadium basically came undone on that one. See, that was back in the day when college football was actually a barrel of fun. Players could celebrate their touchdowns and other exploits with free will. Today, they would be flagged for unsportsmanlike conduct, tossed from the game, tried by a military tribunal, and sent to a maximum security prison for such horrifying transgressions. When Fox flipped, Norton turned to us—remember, he's from Canada, where the field is 110 yards long and you get three downs to make 10 yards—and asked, "Does everyone do that after scoring on a punt return down here?" No, Norton. We'd never seen it before. We wish we could see it again, but that won't happen as long as the NCAA is in charge. (Good grief, return the color to the game!)

Those 21 points were more than enough to send the Badgers packing, and they were achieved in about three and half minutes. Game over, but, hey, let's keep playing.

Okay, then. The Buckeyes drove 89 yards in 14 plays (Johnson, seven-yard run: 28–0). Ohio State recovered a fumble at the Wisconsin 24 (Archie Griffin, 10-yard run: 35–0). Again, Wisconsin fumbled on its 24 (enter the second team, and Lou Williott—Lou *Who?*—powered in from the 7: 42–0). The Buckeyes later drove from their own 27 to score again (Jeff Logan, 16-yard run: 49–0). A horrible punt snap by the Badgers landed the ball at their own 1 (Rod Gerald, subbing for

Greene as all they starters long since had been pulled, scored from there: 56–0). Let the Victory Bell sound!

After the game, all Hayes really would say was, "I think we played well, but the other team made so many mistakes, you can't really tell." Uh-huh.

As for Norton, he was all smiles, feeling as if he has just seen the Super Bowl. Sorry, Norton, nothing of the sort. See, the NFL (No Fun League) would have executed Fox had he done that flip in one of its games.

No. 6: November 2, 1985 vs. Iowa

IOWA	0	7	0	6	**13**
OHIO STATE	5	10	0	7	**22**

If someone wants to fight me in my own backyard, he had better bring an army with him.

—OSU linebacker Chris Spielman

Oh, brother. Here comes Iowa with college football's top passer, Heisman Trophy candidate Chuck Long, and a No. 1 ranking. National TV. Under the lights. Rain. Crappy surface. What the hell are we gonna do? We're gonna play the game, that's what we're gonna do.

True enough, Ohio State had puh-lenty to fear with the Hawk-eyes in the 'Shoe. The Buckeyes defense (with the exception of all-everything linebackers Chris Spielman and Pepper John-son) to that point of the season had injected not much fear into, well, not a single human being on the face of the Earth.

But the Buckeyes were winning and within reach of first place in the Big Ten Conference.

So on this day, with an impassioned pregame speech delivered by tailback Keith Byars, who was being held out with a banged-up foot, as the fuel, the Buckeyes became, well, a different team. "We were underdogs in Ohio Stadium," Spielman would say later to the *Columbus Dispatch*.

Kicker Rich Spangler got things started with a 28-yard field goal, capping an eight-play, 58-yard, first-quarter drive, helped by Jim Karsatos' passes of 19 and 21 yards to Cris Carter and 21 yards to Mike Lanese. Later in the quarter, Sonny Gordon raced in untouched to block and Iowa punt out of the end zone for a safety. What was that? *That* was Ohio State leading the top-ranked team in the nation 5–0 after one quarter.

In the second quarter, OSU made quick work of its next scoring opportunity, which came after William White intercepted Long at the OSU 30 and returned it eight yards. John Wooldridge, subbing for Byars, shortly thereafter jetted 57 yards to the end zone to make it 12–0. Rain? What rain? Hawkeyes coach Hayden Fry was squirming and also grimacing behind his transitional lenses.

Then, Greg Rogan got into the theft act, intercepting Long at midfield and moving it four yards to the 46. George Cooper ripped off runs of 15 and 12 yards, setting the stage for Spangler to kick a 26-yard field goal to make it 15–0.

But Iowa was undaunted. It had five minutes before halftime to get back into the game, and the Hawkeyes went off

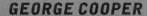
OHIO STATE

GEORGE COOPER

George *Who*? Cooper. George Cooper, one among the stable of bruising backs for Ohio State. With Keith Byars sitting this one out with an injury, the fullback seized the opportunity to make his mark in competition with John Wooldridge and Vince Workman. Cooper ran for 104 yards on 17 carries and had the huge block that sprung Wooldridge for his 57-yard touchdown. On that block, he sent the Hawkeyes' linebacker nearly out of Franklin County.

on a 14-play, 88-yard drive that ate all but 28 seconds of the remaining time. By that point, Ronnie Harmon had put Iowa on the board with a three-yard run to close to within 15–7.

After each team laid a goose egg in the third quarter, the final segment of the game was as dramatic as it could be. After Fred Ridder recovered an Iowa fumble at the Hawkeyes' 31, the Buckeyes needed just five plays to score. Vince Workman's four-yard run through a gaping hole on the left side put the Buckeyes up 22–7, at which point all hell seemed to break loose in the 'Shoe. The Buckeyes gave up an 80-yard drive on eight plays, allowing a two-yard run by David Hudson, but that was that. Splish, splash. No. 1 takes a bath!

As for Spielman, the leader of his own army, the linebacker finished with 19 tackles, one tackle for loss and two, count 'em, two interceptions of Long. "All year long our defense has been criticized," he said. "I don't care what people say. We're 7–1."

So was, by the way, Iowa, which was tied for first in the conference with the Buckeyes after this beating. Said Spielman:

"When we play our best, we can play with anybody in the country. We controlled [running back] Ronnie Harmon and Chuck Long. We had to do that."

No. 7: October 28, 1989 vs. Minnesota

OHIO STATE	0	8	10	23	**41**
MINNESOTA	17	14	0	6	**37**

Coach John Cooper was fond of saying after close games, "We dodged a bullet there." Never was his line more apropos than after this game. Ohio State slogged out of the Metrodome tunnel and promptly put itself at a 31–0 deficit. Yes. Against Minnesota. Seriously, 31 points behind the Gophers? Yes, seriously. But what had unraveled in a heartbeat began to put itself back together. It wasn't easy, though.

Lady (Dumb) Luck struck early and often against the Buckeyes. In the first quarter, a Minnesota punt bounced off the leg of Ohio State's Rich Huffman and was recovered by Scott Streiff of the Golden Gophers. Four plays and 28 yards later, the last on Darrell Thompson's 12-yard run, the Gophers were up 7–0 with just a bit more than 12 minutes left in the first quarter. With 4:17 left in the quarter, Brent Berglund hit a 30-yard field goal to finish off a six-play, nine-yard drive, this courtesy of OSU quarterback Greg Frey's fumble at the Buckeyes' 22-yard line that was recovered by Minnesota's Bob Coughlin. (You remember Frey, a leftover from the Earle Bruce days. Cooper, upon his arrival in Columbus from Arizona State, told anyone who would listen to him that he could win with Frey at the controls.) A holding penalty on fourth-and-goal from the 3 necessitated the field goal. There was

OHIO STATE

TOP 5 OSU PASSING GAMES of ALL-TIME

1. **Art Schlichter** | 458 yards | 1981
   31-for-52 | 36–27 (L) vs. Florida State

2. **Joe Germaine** | 378 yards | 1997
   29-for-43 | 31–27 (L) at Penn State

3. **Greg Frey** | 362 yards | 1989
   20-for-31 | 41–37 (W) at Minnesota

4. **Bobby Hoying** | 354 yards | 1995
   24-for-35 | 28–25 (W) at Penn State

5. **Joe Germaine** | 351 yards | 1998
   31-for-45 | 38–7 (W) at Indiana

at least some hope among the Buckeyes faithful, OSU having survived two disastrous mistakes to trail only 10–0. On the very next series, however, Mike Sunvold of the Gophers swooped in and hammered Frey on third-and-goal at the Minnesota 8. The ball went skyward, whereupon Minnesota's Sean Lumpkin gathered it in and raced 85 yards for a touchdown, putting the Gophers up 17–0. *This isn't really happening, it is? Uh, yep, it is.*

The second quarter brought more misery than any OSU fan should have to suffer. Minnesota snapped off a four-play, 73-yard scoring drive that took only 1:40. Quarterback Scott Schaffner found Steve Rhem for a 29-yard scoring strike after earlier hooking up with Paul Hopewell for 24 yards on the drive. Nausea. Misery. 24–0. Pathetic in every way. And the rout *really* was on after the Gophers picked off a Frey pass and drove 44 yards in nine plays, finished off by Schaffner's five-yard toss to Chris Gaiters. 31–0. The Gophers and their fans were having quite a time. The Buckeyes, to quote president Gordon Gee from more recent times, were looking like and playing like the Little Sisters of the Poor. However, an ounce of redemption could possibly prove to be worth a pound of cure, as the Buckeyes offense finally got its heretofore pathetic engine roaring on a 10-play, 80-yard scoring drive with 10 seconds left in the half. After Frey passed to Bobby Olive for 30 yards, Carlos Snow barreled in from the 1, and Frey hit Jeff Graham for the two-point conversion. 31–8. It might not have happened had Minnesota not been called for illegal substitution on an OSU punt, keeping the march alive. *Hey, we're only down 23 points. Yep, and I'm the Easter Bunny.*

This was, clearly, a tale of two halves. Whatever was said in the locker room at halftime was proper tonic, because the Buckeyes came out after the break with what seemed to be a renewed sense of purpose. Never had Ohio State faced a deficit of this proportion and come back to win the game.

In the third quarter, the Buckeyes reeled off a 66-yard, 11-play drive, finishing with a Pat O'Morrow field goal from 25 yards with 10 minutes left in the third quarter. Frey found his passing stride on the drive, combining with Jim Palmer for 13 yards and Graham for 29 and nine yards. 31–11. *Maybe we're getting somewhere, or…maybe I should take out the trash.* Then OSU plowed through an 11-play, 98-yard drive topped off by Frey's 15-yard pass to Snow with 20 seconds left in the third. 31–18. *Huh. Maybe I'm not the Easter Bunny. Maybe we can win this.*

But Minnesota found something at the start of the fourth quarter, a 32-yard Berglund field goal to finish off a nine-play, 37-yard drive. Schaffner actually fooled the OSU defense on third-and-7 with an 18-yard run to keep things going. 34–18. *Two steps forward, one step back? Lookin' like it.* Then, on the next drive, facing a third-and-8 from the Minnesota 44, Frey found Greg Beatty for 17 yards to keep the drive going, allowing the quarterback to connect with Snow for a 27-yard touchdown and then a two-point conversion to close to within 34–26. *I'm feelin' it now.* I knew we'd come back. (Sure I did.) Then, *boom!* Frey couldn't handle an errant center snap (which looked like it could be heading for the Teflon dome over the field), and Minnesota recovered at the, uh, 32-friggin'-yard line of Ohio State. Lumpkin. Again. But, the defense rose up mightily and unbelievably to force a 42-yard field goal by Berglund with 5:15 to go. 37–26. *I...think...I'm...gonna...hurl.* As Dandy Don Meredith (RIP) would sing years earlier on *Monday Night Football*, "Turn out the lights, the party's over." Not so fast, Gopher breath! The Buckeyes stitched together a three-minute drive that covered 68 yards in eight plays. With 3:04 left, Frey got in from the 1 and then hit Graham for the critical two-point conversion. 37–34. *Gee whiz. I feel just great! Stop them, get the ball back, drive down the field for the winning score, or at least get O'Morrow in there for a field goal to tie. I like our chances.* Well, we stopped them. Cold. And then we took over at our 27 with 1:52 to play. First, Frey found Snow for 18 yards and then Brian Stablein for 19. Frey was slammed down for a 13-yard sack by Skeeter Akre, and he then rebounded with a 34-yard strike to Palmer. We were now at their 15, and there was less than a minute left. No matter, Frey, working from the pocket, coolly delivered a 15-yard laser to Graham to cap the five-play, 73-yard drive.

Sealed: the greatest comeback victory ever, tied with Maryland's 1984 vanquishing of Miami. Frey was a golden boy in the second half after that disastrous first half. He completed 18 of 23 passes for 327 yards, three touchdowns, and three two-point conversions. Again, that's *in a half.* That's a Hall of Fame game in the NFL, folks.

OSU, indeed, had dodged a bullet.

Said Graham, "There was no panic in the huddle.... I knew we would come back.... Some call it luck. Others might call it a miracle. I believe in miracles."

Gracious in defeat, Gophers coach John Gutekunst told the Associated Press, "Let's credit Ohio State. That's a veteran football team, and they deserve a great deal of credit. To come back from 31 down on the road is a real tribute to their players and their staff. I mean that honestly and openly."

Ditto, Schaffner: "You've got to admire their guys for not giving up. We couldn't put them away. That's the difference right there, that those guys wouldn't give up."

No. 8: January 1, 1997, Rose Bowl

OHIO STATE	7	0	7	6	**20**
ARIZONA STATE	0	7	3	7	**17**

To go out and win it the way we did.... We're at the back door of Hollywood, and I don't think they could have come up with a better script.

—OSU linebacker Ryan Miller

Ten years earlier, Ohio State coach John Cooper had led Arizona State to a thrilling victory against Michigan in this game. In the weeks that followed that victory, he was being courted by Columbus to replace the deposed Earle Bruce. Until this game, he hadn't been back. And let us tell you, folks in Buckeye Nation were getting restless. However, here we are again in the Granddaddy of Them All.

The Buckeyes jumped out to a 7–0 first-quarter lead, courtesy of a nine-yard pass to David Boston from Stanley Jackson with 5:04 to play. Jackson was mostly brilliant on the drive, passing eight yards to Dee Miller to convert a third-and-3 from the Buckeyes' 47 and later running for 19 yards to the Sun Devils' 26. On the other side, the OSU defense was having its way. Was this finally going to be a long-overdue thrashing of a Pac-10 opponent under the glare of national television and a packed house? Well, maybe.

The second quarter dawned with Arizona State having a renewed sense of purpose. The Sun Devils methodically marched 80 yards in 13 plays in just less than five minutes,

A SUN DEVIL WE LOVE

Among the noteworthy players on the Arizona State side was linebacker Pat Tillman. In this game, he was an animal with six solo tackles and 11 overall. This is the same Pat Tillman who decided to forego continuing a lucrative NFL career to enter the armed forces and serve his nation. He died by friendly fire in Afghanistan. Rest in peace, Pat Tillman.

scoring when Ricky Boyer hauled in a 25-yard pass from Jake "the Snake" Plummer. The OSU defense was starting to buckle. Worries flooded Scarlet and Gray minds the world over.

With a listless rest of the first half by both teams, our initial thought (hope?) for a thrashing seemed so distant. Uh, it was. This one was going to more resemble a chess match—or a heavyweight title fight—than anything else.

Enter Fred Pagac, the former Buckeyes tight end and line-backers coach who now was a first-season defensive coordinator for OSU. He came up with pressure schemes to keep Plummer confused. There were stunts, blitzes, bull rushes… all of it enough to get what arguably was one of the top three quarterbacks in the nation off balance. He of the slippery stride and split-second decision-making prowess all of a sudden seemed to be running for his life in waist-deep mud. And his teammates at skill positions didn't fare much better for a time. Remember this statistic? 12-for-43? That's 12 tackles by the OSU defense (the "Silver Bullets") for 43 yards in losses. And Pagac had Shawn Springs all but draped over all-everything ASU wideout Keith Poole, who would end the day with one measly catch for 10 measly yards.

The Sun Devils, though, would forge a 10–7, third-quarter lead on a 37-yard field goal to cap a nine-play, 35-yard drive. And then Cooper turned to the two-headed quarterback system he deployed earlier in the season, calling on Arizona native Joe Germaine to get things going as Jackson was struggling. (You think this didn't mean something to Germaine? He wasn't even recruited by ASU, the dumb asses!) With the drive beginning at his own 12, Germaine coolly connected with receiver Dimitrious Stanley on a 72-yard pass play for touchdown and a 14–10 lead. "There was a lot of green in front of me," Stanley would say later. The drive took all of 49 seconds. A two-minute offense in the third quarter.

The intensity ramped up, Plummer struck next. He capped a 58-yard, 10-play drive (on which he was sacked, harried, and otherwise hassled) with a fourth-down, 11-yard run to paydirt. Suddenly, it wasn't looking too promising for the Buckeyes.

There was 1:40 left and more pressure than the Three Mile Island cooling towers could handle. And there was Germaine. Don't forget about Germaine. First, though, Matt Keller brought the Arizona State kickoff back to the Ohio State 35. Most everyone in the free world was hoping for a field goal and overtime, when we would see which team had *any* energy left. Joe Germaine was not "most everyone." He calmly connected with Stanley on pass completions of 11, 13, and 12 yards. Suddenly, the Buckeyes were at the Arizona State 29. Worst-case scenario: a 46-yard field-goal attempt by Josh Jackson, and he could make it. That's the great thing about worst-case scenarios, though: sometimes you needn't have considered them. This was one of those times. First came a pass-interference call against Arizona State, putting the ball at the Sun Devils' 19. Then came *another* pass-interference call (yes!). Suddenly, we're not thinking Jackson any longer (sorry, Josh). Suddenly, Ohio State is at the 5-friggin'-yard line. As the ball was snapped, Stanley took off on a slant, and Germaine looked his way. But Stanley was double-teamed as he neared the end zone. So Germaine turned the other way and zeroed in on wideout David Boston, who snared the pass and danced into the end zone. Buckeyes 20, Sun Devils 17.

Said OSU linebacker Ryan Miller to the *Columbus Dispatch*, "The offense had been slowed down a little bit [only three field goals against Michigan], but this week in practice they've been coming at us. We had a lot of confidence in them. A minute and 40 seconds. That's a lot of time for an offense to try to march down the field. Everyone was really confident in what Joe was going to do."

No. 9: January 2, 2006, Fiesta Bowl

OHIO STATE	7	14	3	10	**34**
NOTRE DAME	7	0	6	7	**20**

> *You just don't give Charlie Weis more than two weeks to prepare for any team. Do it, and your team is in trouble.*
> —Anonymous talking head on an anonymous all-sports network (we're not out to embarrass anyone, other than Notre Dame, that is)

Charlie Weis. The first-year coach of the Fighting Irish. Fresh off an NFL career than previously had him as the offensive mastermind of the New England Patriots Super Bowl champions. The guy who "rescued" Notre Dame from Ty Willingham. The guy who made Columbus native–turned-traitor Brady Quinn into a household name. Talk, talk, talk. In the end, it's kinda cheap, you know?

So here were two 9–2 teams facing off in the Fiesta Bowl, when, really, both teams were just a couple successful plays away from meeting in the Rose Bowl for the national championship. Ohio State had lost by three points to Texas in the waning moments earlier in the season, and Notre Dame had failed similarly against Southern Cal. Well, guess what. Southern Cal and Texas, ranked first and second in the nation, respectively, would make the Rose a game to remember.

This matchup, however, would prove more memorable for the Scarlet and Gray faithful. Few outside Buckeye Nation really considered OSU much of a threat to the Fighting Irish, and after Notre Dame took a 7–0 lead on a 20-yard run by Darius Walker, it certainly seemed that way. Admit it, it did, right? Well, possibly until Ted Ginn Jr. hauled in a 56-yard strike from Troy Smith, who, at the time, was cementing his candidacy for the next season's Heisman Trophy—which, of course, he won. Six plays, 86 yards, *what?* In the second quarter, Ginn was at it again. Coach Jim Tressel, with an ample amount of time of his own to prepare for Notre Dame, saw something… and he caught the Fighting Irish semi-napping. He dialed up a reverse by Ginn, whose world-class speed took him from the far right to a handoff from Smith to a nifty maneuver and a jet-like sprint down the left sideline for a 68-yard touchdown. Big players make big plays on big days. *Big* cliché, but it's true…at least it was on this day. That would make the score, uh, 14–7, *your* Ohio State Buckeyes.

With less than two minutes to go before the half, Smith and Santonio Holmes hooked up for an 85-yard stunner, and the Buckeyes entered the locker room at the half up 21–7.

Eventually in the second half, Quinn would perform as touted, moving his team up and down the field, allowing Walker to

(BAD) LUCK OF THE IRISH?

With its 34–20 defeat at the hands of Ohio State in the 2006 Fiesta Bowl, Notre Dame had secured its record eighth-consecutive bowl loss. Meanwhile, Notre Dame quarterback Brady Quinn's eventual brother-in-law, A.J. Hawk, the Buckeyes' All-America linebacker, led a parade of six Ohio State players into the first round of the ensuing National Football League draft. Okay, genius, name the other four. And for extra credit, name the team by which each was chosen.

ANSWERS:
Donte Whitner (DB), Buffalo; Santonio Holmes (WR), Pittsburgh; Nick Mangold (C),
New York Jets; and Bobby Carpenter (LB), Dallas.

OHIO STATE

score his second touchdown of the game, while the Fighting Irish defense began to make life miserable for the Buckeyes. After a pair of OSU field goals pushed the score to 27–13, it was Walker, again, helping the Fighting Irish to close to within 27–20. And somewhere up there, Woody Hayes overturned his desk and started tearing phone books in half. No matter. With the Buckeyes facing third-and-5 at their own 40, trying to burn clock, Antonio Pittman scorched Notre Dame with a 60-yard touchdown sprint. Pop the top on the bubbly. This one's over—OSU 34, ND 20.

Maybe Weis should have a talk with his defense? Ohio State had a Fiesta Bowl–record 27 first downs. The Buckeyes' 617 yards were third-most in the bowl's history.

After the game, Ohio State linebacker A.J. Hawk had a talk with the national media. "I'd been hearing a lot about, 'How are you guys going to beat a Notre Dame team when you give

Charlie Weis four weeks to prepare for it?' That kind of upset me because I thought, *What about giving Coach Tressel four weeks to prepare for* you?"

Oh, and the quarterbacks? Look at the stats, which do not lie:

Smith:	19-of-28	342 yards	2 TDs	0 INTs
Quinn:	29-of-45	286 yards	0 TDs	0 INTs

No. 10: January 1, 2010: Rose Bowl

OHIO STATE	10	6	3	7	**26**
OREGON	0	10	7	0	**17**

Different season. Different bowl game. Different approach. Different result. Same quarterback.

And so it went on this day for Terrelle Pryor of Ohio State. The previous year in the Fiesta Bowl beatdown by Texas, Coach Jim Tressel had allowed Pryor just 13 pass attempts. This time, Pryor had a night to remember. We'll get to the gaudy stats, but bear in mind the sophomore quarterback ended this game with, to date, career highs in pass attempts, completions, and yards. It was the type of gritty performance Buckeye Nation long had been expecting—he led the OSU offense to 41 minutes, 37 seconds of possession!—and what we thought would happen against Oregon. Pryor's performance justified the hype.

"I think he wanted to have a game that puts him out there in the national ranks, puts him on the map," said Ohio State receiver Dane Sanzenbacher. "You could see it with Terrelle in the huddle.

He kept his poise and kept us moving. It's something we see in practice all the time, but everybody else can see it now, too."

Pryor completed 23 of 37 passes for 266 yards and two touchdowns. He also ran for 72 yards on 20 carries, despite a small tear in the posterior ligament of his left knee.

The Buckeyes opened the game at their own 26. On third-and-6, Pryor dashed 24 yards to the Oregon 46 and a first down. Then, on second-and-6 from the 42, he found DeVier Posey for 11 yards and a first down. Brandon Saine then ran 11 yards for a first down at the Ducks' 13. Pryor tried Sanzenbacher and Posey, with both passes ending in incompletions, and then Saine powered his way 13 yards for a touchdown. The Buckeyes were up 7–0.

After Posey made a fair catch of a less-than-fair Oregon punt at the 50, Pryor and Saine hooked up on a 46-yard pass play for a first down at the Ducks' 4. Three plays, including a fumble, resulted in Devin Barclay's fourth-down field goal of 19 yards. OSU, 10, UO, 0.

In the second quarter, there wasn't really a lot of fireworks from either side, although the Ducks got on the board with a 24-yard field goal to make it 10–3, and LeGarrette Blount found the end zone from three yards out to tie it at 10. It appeared it would be scoreless the rest of the way, but then Pryor dove the Buckeyes into field-goal position, and Barclay connected on a 30-yarder with 1:05 remaining in the half to make it 13–10 Buckeyes. A little breathing room. And more: the Buckeyes got the ball back, and Tressel called on Aaron

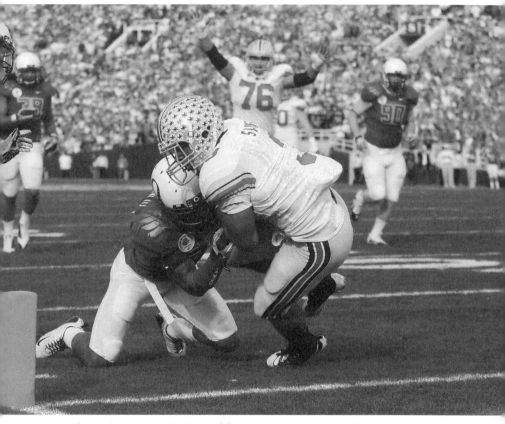

The Buckeyes' Brandon Saine (3) scores on a 13-yard pass from Terrelle Pryor during the 2010 Rose Bowl against Oregon. Ohio State beat the highly touted Jeremiah Masoli and his Ducks 26–17.

Pettrey to attempt a 45-yarder, which was *good*, giving the Buckeyes a 16–10 cushion at the break.

The third quarter brought a massive case of the uh-ohs, as Oregon quarterback Jeremiah Masoli bulled in from one yard out to give the Ducks their first lead at 17–16. It would be Oregon's last truly significant drive of the game. About four

and a half minutes later, Barclay put the Buckeyes back ahead
19–17 on a 38-yarder, and then the defense went into serious
overdrive, allowing Ohio State's offense the time it needed to
salt this one away.

Ohio State was clinging to a two-point lead in the fourth quarter, but Pryor took charge on an 81-yard, 13-play march that
consumed six-plus minutes of clock. Pryor connected with
tight end Jake Ballard on a third-and-13 play at their own 45
with about nine minutes to go. Ballard, at 6'6", leapt out of
a crowd to haul in the pass from a scrambling Pryor. After
another third-down conversion, wide receiver DeVier Posey,
never taking his eye off the ball and changing directions twice,
made a monumental haul-in of a Pryor pass and bounced into
the end zone. It was Ohio State 26, Oregon 17, and the Buckeyes defense would keep it that way the rest of the game.

The Ohio State defense kept the Ducks' high-octane offense
off the field for all but 18:23 of the 60-minute duel. In the end,
the Buckeyes D had so thoroughly frustrated Oregon, and the
Ducks ended up with 20 points and about 200 yards less than
what they had averaged entering this game.

"When I saw him in high school, he was a man amongst boys,
and at times tonight, he looked like a man amongst boys,"
Oregon coach Chip Kelly, who recruited Pryor in Jeannette,
Pennsylvania, and was in his first year as the head Duck, told
national media after the game. "He certainly beat us on how
he threw the ball."

"Definitely the whole night we were just a little bit off," said
Masoli, who was 9-for-20 passing for a measly 81 yards. "We

didn't really open up the playbook regarding the air attack. I don't know why. I wasn't calling the plays." You sure weren't, son. And after "personal problems" surfaced, you left Oregon and landed at the University of Mississippi where *none* of Eli Manning's passing records are in jeopardy.

"I just wanted to come out and show I can be a complete quarterback," Pryor said afterward. "I just wanted to show the world I could wing it like all the other quarterbacks in college football."

Tressel had exactly that in mind as the Buckeyes turned to a different section of the heretofore conservative playbook. "We felt we really needed to come in flinging it around," he said of the amped-up passing attach. "[Pryor] not only made good decisions as to who to go to, he made good decisions when to throw it away and when to step up and run. He was engaged in the game, talking in the game between series…knew what they were doing and why."

Honorable Mention: September 1, 2007

APPALACHIAN STATE	7	21	3	3	**34**
MICHIGAN	14	3	9	6	**32**

You know what? Truthfully, if not quite privately, we liked Lloyd Carr and still do. That's probably puts us on thin ice with Buckeye Nation, but listen to this: Steve had occasion to chat him up while he and Carr were on respective family vacations at Hilton Head Island, South Carolina, one summer. They crossed paths on a morning beach walk at low tide. Feeling something like a gatecrasher, Steve reluctantly said, "Good morning, Coach," stuck his hand out, and Carr took it, shook it, and smiled. Steve had respected Carr for his class and dignity in a world gone sour with player egos, fat TV contracts, and endorsement deals, and he passed along that sentiment. Carr just wanted to coach football. The ensuing chat lasted all of about five minutes, whereupon they resumed their walks in different directions.

So, some years later, while Steve was on a sailing vessel on the Chesapeake Bay on September 1, 2007, he was flattened by the news (gotta love satellite TV afloat, eh?) that Michigan had just lost to heavy underdog App State. (We guess there *is* an app for that. Huh.) Look, we root for the Big Ten (Twelve?) teams...until we play them. We always want Michigan undefeated and ranked No. 1 when we play them, the better to spoil something really terrific; it doesn't happen often, but we take what we can get around here. Our guess is, most of the 110,000 fans at the Big House had no idea exactly where Appalachian State was based (Boone, North Carolina), and the Big Ten's images were turned upside-down by this one. Look at it this way: what proved good for the goose was goose droppings for the gander. Steve recalls a sort of private hurting for Carr, who said something to the effect that his team wasn't prepared for that game and that he took total responsibility for the loss.

Whatever, the unthinkable happened, and it was arguably the biggest upset in the history of college football, at least in modern times. No Division I-FCS team (formerly I-AA) had ever beaten a ranked Division I-FBS team. The Wolverines had entered the game at No. 5 ("had" being the operative word). It was another way that Michigan pissed us off, because now there would be no chance of Ohio State meeting a top-ranked and undefeated Michigan team in the last game of the regular season, which instantly had become irregular.

* * *

SIDE NOTE: We would like to thank the Michigan administration for firing Carr and giving us RichRod. What a gift to Buckeyes fans everywhere! Very generous. Very much appreciated. But now with RichRod in the unemployment line, as of this writing, we were earnestly hoping that a "Michigan man" would become the next head coach. That would mean a renewed emphasis on this rivalry, and it needs it. These blowouts are becoming ho-hum affairs. Alas, we get former Ball State and San Diego State coach Brady Hoke. And that brings to mind these: Joke. Choke. Broke. Smoke—it *is* Ann Arbor, after all. Looks like we're off and running.

3

PLAYERS WE LOVE

WITH SEVEN HEISMAN TROPHIES (including the only player to ever win it *twice*), 183 All-Americans, 69 players selected in the first round of the NFL Draft, eight Pro Football Hall of Famers, and hundreds of players who've played in the NFL, Ohio State has more than its fair share of players to love.

ARCHIE GRIFFIN

It was the classic story of a hometown boy makes good. But in this case, the hometown boy makes *great*!

Columbus' own Archie Griffin was a high school star at East-moor High School and entered Ohio State in 1972. However, when Griffin fumbled on the first carry of his freshman season, many Buckeyes fans thought that his coach, Woody Hayes, would be reluctant to give the freshman back another chance very soon. However, the next game, Griffin rushed for a school-record 239 yards.

Archie Griffin dashes toward the end zone during a game against Illinois on November 2, 1974, in Columbus. The 22-yard run put Griffin over 100 yards rushing for the 18th straight game, setting one of the two-time Heisman Trophy winner's many college records.

TOP 5 RUSHING YARDS (CAREER)

		Att.	Yards	Years
1.	Archie Griffin	924	5,589	1972–1975
2.	Eddie George	683	3,768	1992–1995
3.	Tim Spencer	644	3,553	1979–1982
4.	Chris Wells	585	3,382	2006–2008
5.	Keith Byars	619	3,200	1982–1985

OHIO STATE

He ran for 867 yards in his freshman season, then exploded the following year with 1,577 yards. He improved to 1,695 yards as a junior and capped his illustrious career with 1,450 yards as a senior. He led the Big Ten in rushing three consecutive seasons; in his four-year career, he ran for an NCAA record 5,589 yards (since broken). He rushed for 100-plus yards in an NCAA record 31 consecutive games. The Buckeyes were 40–5–1 with Griffin as a starter. He is one of just two players in history to start four Rose Bowl games.

He won the Heisman Trophy following his junior season (1974), then became the only player in history to win the award twice by winning it again as a senior in 1975.

Griffin was inducted into the College Football Hall of Fame in 1986. His uniform No. 45 was retired in 1999. He was ranked No. 21 on ESPN's greatest college football players list in 2007.

THE GREATEST, ACCORDING TO WOODY

"Who is the greatest track man in history? Why, it's Jesse Owens! He won so many gold medals that Hitler left the stadium in Berlin because he didn't want to recognize that this great athlete from Ohio State was superior. And who is the greatest college football player? Why, it's Arch [Griffin]. Nobody else in the history of football has ever won two Heisman trophies. And who is the greatest golfer of all time? Why, it's Jack Nicklaus. Nobody can touch him. He's the best. And who is the greatest in basketball? Why, it's John Havlicek. He's Mr. Basketball."

—Woody Hayes

Griffin was a first-round pick in the 1976 NFL Draft and played seven seasons with the Cincinnati Bengals. He rushed for 2,808 yards, caught 192 passes for 1,607 yards, and played in Super Bowl XVI against the 49ers. He ended his pro career by playing with the Jacksonville Bulls of the USFL for one season.

Today, Griffin is head of The Ohio State University Alumni Association. He continues to speak to the OSU football team before every game, and—more good news for Buckeyes fans—Archie's son, Adam, signed with Ohio State in 2010.

TROY SMITH

Nothing came easy for Troy Smith. At the age of three, he and his two siblings were moved by his mother from Columbus to Cleveland. At nine, he moved in with foster parents and played youth league football. In high school at St. Edward in Lakewood, Ohio, he was thrown off the basketball team after he elbowed an opponent in the head. He transferred to Glenville High School in Cleveland, where his football coach was Ted Ginn Sr. (At Glenville, Smith teamed with wide receiver Ted Ginn Jr., who also played with him at Ohio State and with the San Francisco 49ers.)

Smith accepted the final scholarship that Ohio State had to offer in 2002. He redshirted his initial season, then played little as a running back and kick returner in 2003. The following year, he entered the season as the No. 2 quarterback, behind Justin Zwick. When Zwick went down with an injury midway through the 2004 season, Smith got the call and led the Buckeyes to wins in four of their final five regular season games. However, when Smith reportedly accepted $500 from a booster, he was suspended from playing in the 2004 Alamo Bowl and the opening game of the 2005 season.

Smith picked up where he left off the previous season. In 2005 he threw for 2,282 yards and 16 touchdowns, while throwing just four interceptions. He also rushed for 611 yards and 11 TDs. The Buckeyes finished at 10–2, concluding the season with a 34–20 win over Notre Dame in the Fiesta Bowl.

In 2006 Smith threw for 2,542 yards and 30 touchdowns (with just six interceptions). He also rushed for 204 yards and one TD in leading the Buckeyes to a 12–1 record and a spot in the BCS National Championship Game.

Smith won the Heisman Trophy, taking 86.7 percent of the first-place votes, an all-time record. Despite his Heisman Trophy and impressive statistics, Smith wasn't chosen until the

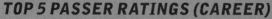

OHIO STATE

TOP 5 PASSER RATINGS (CAREER)

		Rating	Years
1.	Troy Smith	157.1	2003–2006
2.	Joe Germaine	151.0	1996–1998
3.	Terrelle Pryor	144.6	2008–2010
4.	Bobby Hoying	142.6	1992–1995
5.	Jim Karsatos	137.2	1983–1986

end of the fifth round in the 2007 NFL Draft, by the Baltimore Ravens. After spending three seasons with the Ravens in a backup role, Smith was released. Two days later, he was picked up by the San Francisco 49ers, where he was thrust into the starting lineup at midseason.

Beside the victories and Heisman Trophy, why is Smith one of our favorite players? His performances against Michigan. In three games against the Wolverines, Smith amassed 1,151 yards of total offense, throwing for seven TDs and running for two more. Ohio State was 3–0, making him the first Buckeyes QB since Tippy Dye from 1934 to 1936 to lead the Buckeyes to three consecutive wins.

EDDIE GEORGE

Okay, we'll get the football-related items out of the way first. Despite an impressive start to his college career, scoring five touchdowns in his first 25 carries as a freshman, Eddie George quickly was sent to the doghouse after fumbling twice inside Illinois' 5-yard line in a loss to the Illini. He was used sparingly the remainder of the season and was the third-string running back as a sophomore. He finally broke into the starting lineup as a junior, rushing for 1,442 yards and 12 touchdowns while leading the Buckeyes to a 9–4 record.

As a senior, he ran for a school record 1,927 yards and 24 TDs. He made amends against the Illini by rushing for a school-record 314 yards and three touchdowns. George won the Heisman Trophy in 1995 in the closest vote in the history of the award at the time. He wound up his Ohio State career as the second leading rusher in school history (3,768 yards) and No. 3 on the career list for rushing touchdowns (44).

He was selected in the first round of the 1996 NFL Draft by the Houston Oilers/Tennessee Titans and was the NFL's Rookie of the Year. He played in four Pro Bowls, scored two touchdowns in Super Bowl XXXIV, and was just the second NFL back to rush for more than 10,000 yards without missing a start.

When he wasn't playing football, George made the most of his time. He married Tamara "Taj" Johnson, an R&B singer and contestant on the reality TV show *Survivor*. George made an appearance on *Survivor* with his wife, then the two of them teamed up on the reality show *I Married a Baller*. George has also appeared on *Nash Bridges*, the MTV show *Made*, in the Steven Seagal movie *Into the Sun*, and the Dwayne Johnson movie *The Game Plan*. He hosted a video-game show, and has worked with FOX Sports on various pregame shows and as a game analyst.

OHIO STATE'S HEISMAN WINNERS

	Position	Year
Les Horvath	Halfback	1944
Vic Janowicz	Halfback	1950
Howard "Hopalong" Cassady	Halfback	1955
Archie Griffin*	Running Back	1974, 1975
Eddie George	Running Back	1995
Troy Smith†	Quarterback	2006

*Only player in NCAA history to win Heisman twice (we hope this two-time honor stands forever)
† Won Heisman vote by largest margin in NCAA history

He opened restaurants in Nashville and Columbus (Eddie George's Grille 27). He is a licensed landscape architect and recently graduated from Northwestern's highly regarded MBA program.

LES HORVATH

Les Horvath thought his college football playing days were over when he helped the Buckeyes beat the Iowa Pre-Flight team 41–12 to complete the 1942 season. He was in graduate school, studying dentistry, when Buckeyes coach Carroll Wid-does approached Horvath and told him about the change in college football eligibility rules due to World War II and the scarcity of able-bodied players.

Horvath returned to the Ohio State team in 1944 and had one of the finest seasons in school history. He led the Buckeyes to a 9–0 record and a No. 2 national ranking, and he won the Heisman Trophy.

Following his Heisman season, Horvath completed his dental training and joined the U.S. Navy. Upon his discharge, he played pro football for three years before embarking on a dental career in Los Angeles.

VIC JANOWICZ

Vic Janowicz experienced extreme highs and extreme lows throughout his life. A native of Elyria, Ohio, he enrolled at Ohio State in 1948. He led the Buckeyes to a 6–3 record in 1950 as a junior tailback in the single-wing offense under Coach Wes Fesler and won the Heisman Trophy. But Fesler departed as the Buckeyes coach and was replaced by Woody Hayes.

TOP 5 RUSHING YARDS IN A SEASON

		Att.	Yards	Year
1.	Eddie George	328	1,927	1995
2.	Keith Byars	336	1,764	1984
3.	Archie Griffin	256	1,695	1974
4.	Chris Wells	274	1,609	2007
5.	Archie Griffin	247	1,577	1973

OHIO STATE

"Vic Janowicz was not only a great runner, but also passed, was a place-kicker and punter, played safety on defense, and was an outstanding blocker. He epitomized the 'triple threat' football player," said Hayes.

Janowicz was also an outstanding baseball player at Ohio State and is one of just two Heisman Trophy winners to play professional football and baseball. (The other is Bo Jackson.) Following his graduation, he opted to pursue a pro baseball career. He made it to the big leagues, but hit just .214 for the Pittsburgh Pirates over two seasons as a backup catcher. The next year, he gave pro football a try. He was the Washington Redskins' starting halfback in 1955, but during camp in 1956, he was involved in an auto accident that caused serious brain damage and left him partially paralyzed.

He eventually made a full recovery, but his athletic career was cut short. He remained a part of the Buckeyes family as a broadcaster and stayed in Columbus to work for a local manufacturing company and the state government.

Janowicz died of cancer in 1996.

HOWARD "HOPALONG" CASSADY

Owning one of the best nicknames in sports history, Howard Albert Cassady became a football legend as a Heisman Trophy winner with the Buckeyes.

A native of Columbus, Cassady enrolled at Ohio State in 1952. As a running back, he scored 37 touchdowns in 36 games and was a consensus All-American in 1954 and 1955. Ohio State was 10–0 and the No. 1 team in the final national polls in 1954. He finished third in the Heisman Trophy voting as a junior, but in 1955, he won the award by the largest margin at the time.

Cassady ended his college career as the school's all-time rushing leader with 2,466 yards (broken by Jim Otis in 1969) and the career scoring leader with 222 points (broken by Pete Johnson in 1975). He also was a star on the baseball field, leading the Buckeyes in home runs in 1955 and stolen bases in 1956.

Cassady played in the NFL for eight years (with Detroit, Cleveland, and Philadelphia), then formed a company that manufactured concrete pipes. He also served as a scout for the New York Yankees and was the first-base coach for the Columbus Clippers.

So where did the name "Hopalong" come from? Columbus sportswriters dubbed Cassady during his first game as a

TOP 5 TDS SCORED (CAREER)

1.	Pete Johnson	58	1973–1976
2.	Keith Byars	50	1982–1985
3.	Eddie George	45	1992–1995
4t.	Tim Spencer	37	1979–1982
	Hopalong Cassady	37	1952–1955

OHIO STATE

freshman at OSU when he scored three touchdowns in a win over Indiana. They said he "hopped all over the field like the fictional cowboy, Hopalong Cassidy."

REX KERN

Most Buckeyes fans know that Rex Kern was a star quarterback for Woody Hayes and the Buckeyes. But did you know that it was OSU's basketball success that brought Kern to the Columbus campus?

As a basketball star at Lancaster High School, Kern had basketball scholarship offers to powers UCLA, North Carolina, and Ohio State. Kern eventually committed to OSU and played both sports as a freshman (when freshmen were ineligible to play on the varsity squad). He was the starting QB of the freshman football team, but while playing basketball, he injured his back. The injury required surgery, but Kern recovered in time to earn the starting QB spot for the football team in 1968, beating out returning starter Bill Long.

Kern directed the offense on the undefeated team that won the national championship. As a junior, the Buckeyes were 8–0 and averaging 46 points a game, but they were derailed by Michigan 24–12. Kern threw four interceptions in that game. The Buckeyes still were Big Ten co-champions and Kern was a first-team All-American. He finished third in the Heisman Trophy balloting.

As a senior, Kern was named the team captain and guided the Buckeyes to another Big Ten title. But Ohio State lost the Rose Bowl to Stanford. Kern wound up fifth in the Heisman

Rex Kern led Ohio State to an undefeated, national championship season in 1968, which included a win over USC in the Rose Bowl. Kern returned the Buckeyes to Pasadena in 1970 and was a finalist for the Heisman Trophy.

voting. Despite his impressive college career, Kern wasn't selected until the 10th round of the 1971 NFL Draft. He never took a snap in his pro career. He was converted to defensive back and played four years before retiring due to injuries.

Kern returned to school, earning a doctorate in education. In 1978 he was selected to the Varsity "O" Hall of Fame, in 2000 he was named to the OSU Football All-Century Team, and in 2007 he was elected to the College Football Hall of Fame.

TOP 5 PASSING YARDS IN A SEASON

		Yards	Year
1.	Joe Germaine	3,330	1998
2.	Bobby Hoying	3,269	1995
3.	Terrelle Pryor	2,772	2010
4.	Art Schlichter	2,551	1981
5.	Troy Smith	2,542	2006

PETE JOHNSON

Pete Johnson was the powerful blocking fullback for Archie Griffin, who set a school record for touchdowns. From 1973 to 1976, Johnson scored 58 touchdowns and ran for 2,308 yards. His top game was against North Carolina in 1975. While Griffin ran for 157 yards, Johnson rushed for 148 yards and scored five touchdowns, an OSU record. His top season was 1975, when he ran for 1,059 yards and scored 26 TDs.

Johnson played eight seasons in the NFL. He spent his first seven seasons with the Cincinnati Bengals and led the team in rushing each year. He was a member of the Bengals' Super Bowl XVI team that lost to San Francisco. He spent his final season with San Diego and Miami. In eight pro seasons, Johnson ran for 5,626 yards, caught 175 passes for another 1,334 yards, and scored 82 TDs.

Since leaving Ohio State, Johnson has had his problems off the field, ranging from drug charges to check fraud. In 2000 he was named to the OSU All-Century Team, and in 2007 he was inducted into the Varsity "O" Hall of Fame.

JIM OTIS

Old friendships can come in handy—especially when it comes to recruiting high school football players. Woody Hayes' roommate at the Sigma Chi fraternity at Denison University was James John Otis. The two remained close friends. James John Otis became a doctor and ran a medical practice in Celina, Ohio. His son, Jim Otis, was a top high school football running back. It didn't take Hayes long to convince the younger Otis that Ohio State was the place he could best use those talents.

Jim Otis led the Buckeyes in rushing from 1967 to 1969. He helped lead the Buckeyes to an undefeated season in 1968 and was a first-team All-America fullback in 1969. He

TOP 5 TDS SCORED IN A SEASON

1.	Pete Johnson	26	1975
2.	Eddie George	25	1995
3.	Keith Byars	24	1984
4.	Keith Byars	22	1983
5.	Champ Henson	20	1972

OHIO STATE

remains second (to Archie Griffin) on Ohio State's career rushing yards–per-game list.

He played nine years in the NFL. His best season was 1975, when he rushed for 1,076 yards with the St. Louis Cardinals and was selected for the Pro Bowl. Otis' son, James John Otis II, walked on at Ohio State in 2001 and lettered for the Buckeyes in 2003 as a special teams player. Another son, Jeff (who attended Columbia), spent four seasons in the NFL with four teams.

BOB FERGUSON

Pete Johnson and Jim Otis get most of the attention in discussing the greatest fullbacks in Ohio State history. But many Buckeyes fans who were around to see him claim that Bob Ferguson was a better fullback than either of them.

Ferguson enrolled at Ohio State in 1958 after playing high school football at Troy, Ohio. When he became eligible in 1959 as a sophomore, he beat out the starting senior fullback, Bob White, who had been touted as a Heisman Trophy candidate. Ferguson led the Buckeyes in rushing that season and averaged 6.1 yards per carry.

In 1960 Ferguson was an All-American. As a senior, he was the "thunder" to halfback Paul Warfield's "lightning" in one of the most explosive backfields in college football history. Ferguson was again an All-American and added the UPI College Player of the Year award and finished second (to Ernie Davis) in the Heisman Trophy vote. The Buckeyes were 8–0–1 in 1961 and were the runner-up for the national championship in both major polls.

In three years, Ferguson ran for 2,162 yards, second in school history at the time. He is the only Buckeyes multiyear starter at back who was never tackled for a loss in his career.

He was a first-round draft pick by the Pittsburgh Steelers in the NFL and the San Diego Chargers in the AFL. He opted to join the Steelers, but was forced to retire after two seasons due to injuries. Ferguson returned to the Ohio State campus and earned a master's degree in sociology. He remained in Columbus and worked as a youth counselor. In 1987 Ferguson was inducted into the Varsity "O" Hall of Fame. In 1996 he was selected to the College Football Hall of Fame. He died in 2004 due to complications with diabetes.

CHARLES "CHIC" HARLEY

We won't attempt to top Buckeye James Thurber's description of Chic Harley. In 1941 Thurber wrote: "If you never saw him run with a football, we can't describe it to you. It wasn't like Red Grange or Tom Harmon or anybody else. It was kind of a cross between music and cannon fire, and it brought your heart up under your ears."

Harley moved from Chicago (hence the nickname "Chic") to Columbus with his family when he was 12 and attended East High School. In 1916 Harley started his football career with the Buckeyes and led them to a 7–0 record. He was a consensus first-team All-American. The following year, the Buckeyes were 8–0–1, and Harley was again an All-American. He missed the 1918 season to serve in the U.S. Army but returned to OSU in time to play in the 1919 season. The Buckeyes were 6–1. The only loss in Harley's career was at the hands of

Illinois on the last play of his last game. But more important, that was the year that OSU beat Michigan for the first time (13–3). Harley again earned All-America honors.

Playing running back, defensive back, kicker, and punter, Harley scored 201 points in his career, a school record that stood until 1955. His 8.7 points per game remains a record. He also holds the unofficial OSU record with four interceptions in the 1919 game against the Wolverines. He also lettered in basketball, baseball, and track. The 1917 OSU baseball team won the conference championship, and he set a conference record in the 50-yard dash.

MOST INTERCEPTIONS IN A GAME

		No.	Opponent	Year
1.	Chic Harley*	4	@ Michigan	1919
2.	Fred Bruney	3	vs. Illinois	1951
	Fred Bruney	3	vs. Michigan	1952
	Arnie Chonko	3	vs. Indiana	1964
	Ted Provost	3	@ Northwestern	1967
	Bruce Ruhl	3	vs. Wisconsin	1974
	Craig Cassady	3	vs. Michigan State	1975
	Mike Guess	3	@ SMU	1977
	William White	3	vs. West Virginia	1987
	Damon Moore	3	@ Iowa	1996

*Unofficial record

OHIO STATE

Harley was one of the original 44 players inducted into the College Football Hall of Fame in 1951. He was the first-team halfback on the AP's all-star team for the first half of the 20th century. He was joined in the backfield by Jim Thorpe. Illinois' Red Grange was second-team. Ohio State retired No. 47 in his honor, and the Touchdown Club of Columbus named its College Football Player of the Year trophy the Chic Harley Award.

Soon after his graduation, Harley was diagnosed with dementia praecox (schizophrenia), and he was a patient at VA hospitals for the remainder of his life. He died in 1974 at the age of 79.

PETE STINCHCOMB

Pete Stinchcomb was Chic Harley's running mate during Ohio State's first win over Michigan in 1919. Stinchcomb didn't receive the accolades that Harley did that season when the Buckeyes were co-champions of the conference, but he was named the All-Western quarterback. The following year, after Harley graduated, all the attention turned to Stinchcomb. He switched to halfback and proceeded to lead the Buckeyes to an undefeated season and their first Rose Bowl appearance. He was a unanimous first-team All-American.

Stinchcomb enrolled at OSU in 1916 and played for the Buckeyes in 1917, 1919, and 1920. He was named All–Big Ten in 1917. But at the onset of World War I, Stinchcomb enlisted in the U.S. Navy and missed the 1918 Ohio State season.

He returned to Columbus to star for the 1919 and 1920 teams. Besides his exploits on the football field, he also played for the

OSU baseball team and competed in the broad jump in track (winning the 1921 NCAA championship). Stinchcomb is also credited with starting the Student Bookstore in 1920.

Following graduation, he played pro football for four seasons before returning to OSU in 1935 as the backfield coach. He was elected to the College Football Hall of Fame in 1973. And Stinchcomb Drive, on campus between Olentangy River Road and Route 315, is named in his honor.

WES FESLER

Wes Fesler was a three-sport star at Ohio State, playing football, basketball, and baseball. From Youngstown, Ohio, Fesler enrolled at Ohio State in 1927, started at the end position, and earned All-America honors in 1928, 1929, and 1930. He was named the Most Valuable Player of the Big Ten Conference in 1930. In 1939 noted sportswriter Grantland Rice listed Fesler on his all-time college football team. In 1954 he was inducted into the College Football Hall of Fame, and he was a charter inductee in the Varsity "O" Hall of Fame in 1977.

In basketball, Fesler was OSU's first consensus first-team All-American, despite the Buckeyes' 4–13 record in 1930–1931.

After graduation, Fesler passed up offers to play professionally and joined the Buckeyes' coaching staff. He was an assistant with the football team for two years before accepting the job as head basketball coach at Harvard. He returned to Ohio State as the head football coach from 1947 to 1950, compiling a 21–13–3 record. His 1949 Buckeyes team was the Big Ten

OSU's THREE-TIME ALL-AMERICANS

Chic Harley	1916, 1917, 1919
Wesley Fesler	1928, 1929, 1930
Lew Hinchman	1930, 1931, 1932
Merle Wendt	1934, 1935, 1936
Archie Griffin	1973, 1974, 1975
Tom Skladany	1974, 1975, 1976
Mike Doss	2000, 2001, 2002
James Laurinaitis	2006, 2007, 2008

OHIO STATE

co-champ and beat California 17–14 in the Rose Bowl, finishing sixth in the nation in the AP's final poll.

WARREN AMLING

Warren Amling is the answer to the trivia question: who is the only member of the College Football Hall of Fame to start an NCAA Final Four basketball game? But there is nothing trivial about Amling's college career at Ohio State. He was a unanimous first-team All-America guard on the Buckeyes' 1945 football team and finished seventh in the Heisman Trophy voting. The following season, Amling moved to tackle and was an All-American again. He was selected to the College Football Hall of Fame in 1984.

In basketball, Amling was a starter in 1945, 1946, and 1947. The Buckeyes were in the NCAA tournament in 1945 and

1946, finishing third in the nation in 1946. Amling passed up a pro football career to enter veterinary medicine school. He established a practice in London, Ohio.

GOMER JONES

Jones was the star of the Ohio State football teams from 1933 to 1935, playing center on offense and linebacker on defense. He was the team captain in 1935 and a consensus All-American. He was the 15th player selected in the 1936 NFL Draft but opted to pursue a coaching career instead.

Jones was a Buckeyes assistant coach from 1936 to 1940, before moving to John Carroll, Nebraska, and Oklahoma. He was an assistant at Oklahoma for 17 years under Bud Wilkinson. The Sooners won national championships in 1950, 1955, and 1956, and set an NCAA record with 47 consecutive wins. When Wilkinson retired in 1964, Jones was named Oklahoma's head coach. His teams were 9–11–1 in two seasons. Jones resigned as head coach but became the school's athletics director, a position he held until his death in 1971. Jones was inducted into the College Football Hall of Fame in 1978.

JIM PARKER

Jim Parker had more success in his three years of football at Ohio State than practically any player in school history. Consider:

- In 1954 he was the top lineman on both sides of the ball as the Buckeyes won the national championship.

OHIO STATE

BUCKEYES PLAYERS IN THE COLLEGE FOOTBALL HALL OF FAME

	Pos.	Played	Inducted
Chic Harley	HB	1916–1917, 1919	1951
Pete Stinchcomb	HB	1917, 1919–1920	1973
Wes Fesler	E	1928–1930	1954
Gomer Jones	C	1933–1935	1978
Gust Zarnas	G	1935–1937	1975
Jim Daniell	T	1939–1941	1977
Les Horvath	HB/QB	1940–1942, 1944	1969
Bill Willis	T	1942–1944	1971
Warren Amling	G/T	1944–1946	1984
Vic Janowicz	HB	1949–1951	1976
Hopalong Cassady	HB	1952–1955	1979
Jim Parker	G	1954–1956	1974
Aurealius Thomas	G	1955–1957	1989
Jim Houston	E	1957–1959	2005
Bob Ferguson	FB	1959–1961	1996
Rex Kern	QB	1968–1970	2007
Jim Stillwagon	G	1968–1970	1991
Jack Tatum	S	1968–1970	2004
John Hicks	T	1970, 1972–1973	2001
Randy Gradishar	LB	1971–1973	1998
Archie Griffin	HB	1972–1975	1986
Chris Spielman	LB	1984–1987	2009

- In 1955 he was the key blocker for Howard "Hopalong" Cassady, the year Cassady won the Heisman Trophy. Parker was a unanimous All-American.
- In 1956 Parker won the Outland Trophy, given to the top collegiate lineman in the nation. He finished eighth in the Heisman Trophy voting.

Parker was the first-round pick of the Baltimore Colts in the 1957 NFL Draft. He spent 11 seasons with the Colts, playing in eight Pro Bowls as an offensive tackle and guard. He became the first full-time offensive lineman inducted into the Pro Football Hall of Fame in 1973, his first year of eligibility. In 1974 Parker was elected to the College Football Hall of Fame, and in 1977 he was a charter member of the Varsity "O" Hall of Fame.

JOHN HICKS

One of the greatest offensive linemen in Buckeyes history was John Hicks. The Outland Trophy winner in 1973, he anchored the Ohio State line in 1970, 1972, and 1973. He was the first player to start in three Rose Bowls and is the last interior lineman to finish second in the Heisman Trophy voting.

Hicks was the lead blocker for Archie Griffin and Pete Johnson as the Buckeyes went 28–3–1 with him in the lineup. (He sat out most the 1971 season with a knee injury.) He was an All-American in 1972 and 1973. He was a first-round draft pick of the New York Giants in 1974 and played four seasons with the Giants before retiring due to injuries. He was elected to the College Football Hall of Fame in 2001.

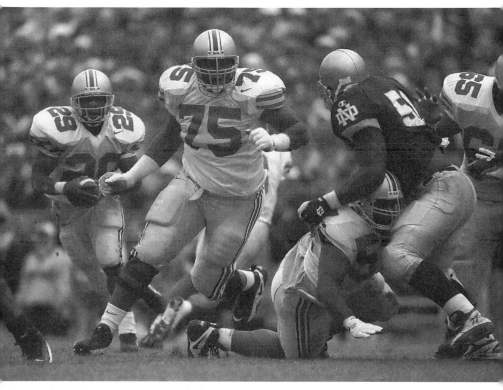

The Buckeyes' Orlando Pace (75) looks to block a Fighting Irish defender for running back Pepe Pearson (29) in Ohio State's 29–16 victory over Notre Dame in South Bend in 1996. Photo courtesy of Getty Images

ORLANDO PACE

Synonymous with the term "pancake block," Orlando Pace was one of the Buckeyes' best offensive linemen ever, and he has the hardware to prove it.

Out of Sandusky High School, Pace was just the second true freshman to start on opening day for the Buckeyes. The tackle won the Lombardi Award in 1995 and 1996 as the top college

OSU LOMBARDI AWARD WINNERS
(BEST LINEMAN OR LINEBACKER)

Jim Stillwagon	1970
John Hicks	1973
Chris Spielman	1987
Orlando Pace	1995
Orlando Pace	1996
A.J. Hawk	2005

OSU OUTLAND TROPHY WINNERS (BEST LINEMAN)

Jim Parker	1956
Jim Stillwagon	1970
John Hicks	1973
Orlando Pace	1996

lineman or linebacker and the Outland Trophy in 1996. He finished fourth in the Heisman Trophy vote in 1996.

He was the first player chosen in the 1997 NFL Draft, becoming the first offensive lineman to go No. 1 since Ron Yary in 1968. Pace played 12 years for the St. Louis Rams and one season with the Chicago Bears. He was selected to seven Pro Bowls, won a Super Bowl, and blocked for three consecutive NFL MVPs (Kurt Warner in 1999 and 2001 and Marshall Faulk in 2000).

In 1999 Pace was named to the *Sports Illustrated* College Football All-Century Team as a starting tackle. Today, Pace has a sports bar in Sandusky and is the spokesperson for several St. Louis–area charities.

JIM STILLWAGON

Jim Stillwagon was a two-time All-America defensive lineman (1969–1970), an Outland Trophy winner (1970), and the first winner of the Lombardi Award (1970). The Mt. Vernon native helped lead the 1968 Ohio State team to an undefeated season and national championship. In 1991 he was named to the College Football Hall of Fame.

Stillwagon was a fifth-round pick in the 1971 NFL Draft but opted to play in the Canadian Football League. He played five seasons up north, earning All-Star honors three years.

BILL WILLIS

Did the Buckeyes really have a 202-pound, two-way lineman who ran the 60- and 100-yard dashes on the track team? Yep.

BUCKEYES PLAYERS IN THE PRO FOOTBALL HALL OF FAME

	Pos.	Team (Yrs.)	Inducted
Lou Groza	OT/K	Cleveland (1946–1959, 1961–1967)	1974
Dante Lavelli	E	Cleveland (1946–1956)	1975
Bill Willis	DL	Cleveland (1946–1953)	1977
Jim Parker	OL	Baltimore Colts (1957–1967)	1973
Dick LeBeau	CB	Detroit (1959–1972)	2010
Paul Warfield	WR	Cleveland (1964–1969, 1976–1977), Miami (1970–1974)	1983

OHIO STATE

It was Bill Willis, a member of the College Football Hall of Fame and Pro Football Hall of Fame.

Buckeyes coach Francis Schmidt had not played any black players during his tenure from 1934 to 1940. An African American, Willis was able to get his chance to star at Ohio State in 1942 when Schmidt was replaced by Paul Brown. Willis helped lead the Buckeyes to the Big Ten title and national championship in 1942. He stayed in Columbus when he failed the U.S. Army physical due to varicose veins and was an all-conference selection in 1943. The following season, the Buckeyes were undefeated, and Willis was named an All-American.

The Columbus native played for Brown and his Cleveland Browns in the All-America Football Conference. The team joined the NFL in 1950, and Willis was invited to play in the Pro Bowl in 1950, 1951, and 1952. Willis' No. 99 uniform was retired by Ohio State in 2007. It was the first time the uniform number of a lineman and a defensive player was retired.

RANDY GRADISHAR

The best linebacker to play for Woody Hayes? According to the coach, it was Randy Gradishar. The Champion (Ohio) High School star played for the Buckeyes from 1971 to 1973. As a senior, Gradishar led the Buckeyes in tackles (134), including 22 in one game (vs. Washington State). Ohio State finished the season with a 10–0–1 record and four shutouts. Gradishar was a two-time All-American and finished sixth in the voting for the Heisman Trophy in 1973. He concluded his college career with 320 tackles, the most in OSU history when he graduated.

Gradishar was a first-round pick of the Denver Broncos in 1974. He played 10 seasons, earning seven Pro Bowl berths and was the NFL Defensive Player of the Year in 1978. His 2,049 career tackles was an NFL record when he retired in 1983. He also had 20 interceptions and 13 fumble recoveries.

Today, Ohio State's annual award for the team's top linebacker is named in honor of Gradishar. He was named to ABC-TV's All-Century Team in 2000.

CHRIS SPIELMAN

Chris Spielman was the national high school scholar-athlete of the year in 1983 at Washington High School in Massillon. He chose Ohio State and made a lasting impression. He was a two-time All-America linebacker and won the Lombardi Award in 1987.

TOP 5 TACKLES IN A SEASON

		No.	Year
1.	Tom Cousineau	211	1978
2.	Chris Spielman	205	1986
3.	Marcus Marek	178	1982
4.	David Adkins	172	1977
5t.	Chris Spielman	156	1987
	Rowland Tatum	156	1983

OHIO STATE

Ohio State defensive back Jack Tatum, nicknamed "the Assassin" for his vicious hits, was the 1970 Defensive Player of the Year and went on to an All-Pro career with the Oakland Raiders.

He played 10 seasons in the NFL for the Detroit Lions and Buffalo Bills. His 1,138 career tackles at Detroit was a team record, and he played in four Pro Bowls. Upon his retirement, he began a broadcasting career with FOX Sports and ESPN. Spielman also tried coaching. He was the head coach of the Columbus Destroyers of the Arena Football League. In his only season (2005), the team finished 2–15. He was elected to the College Football Hall of Fame in 2009.

JACK TATUM

One of the hardest hitters in the history of football, Jack Tatum was a Buckeyes star from 1968 to 1970. "I like to believe that my best hits border on felonious assault," Tatum said.

"The Assassin" was originally recruited as a running back, but assistant coach Lou Holtz convinced Tatum (and Coach Hayes) to make the switch to defensive back. Tatum was an All–Big Ten selection three times, an All-American twice, and was the 1970 national Defensive Player of the Year. In 2004 he was elected to the College Football Hall of Fame. Today, the Buckeyes' weekly award for the "Hit of the Week" is named in Tatum's honor.

As an NFL star with the Oakland Raiders, he is unfortunately most remembered for his hit on New England Patriots wide receiver Darryl Stingley in a 1978 preseason game, which left Stingley paralyzed for life. But among of the highlights of his stellar pro career was setting the NFL record with a 104-yard fumble recovery return in 1972. He retired with 37 career interceptions and 10 fumble recoveries for a combined 900 return yards. Tatum was chosen to three Pro Bowls and started for the world-champion Raiders team that won Super Bowl XI.

Tatum suffered from diabetes and eventually had his right leg amputated and all five toes from his left foot removed. He helped raise the awareness of the disease with his work for the Central Ohio Diabetes Association. He suffered a heart attack in 2010 and died at the age of 61.

VLADE JANAKIEVSKI

Vlade Janakievski was born in Yugoslavia and moved to the U.S. with his parents at the age of 10. He was playing soccer at Ohio State when he walked on to the football team and earned the starting place-kicker spot in 1977. He remained the starter for four years, finishing his career as the second-leading scorer in Buckeyes history (behind Pete Johnson). Janakievski hit 18-of-21 field goals in 1979, connecting on 15

TOP 5 CONSECUTIVE FGS MADE

		FGs	Year(s) (Games)
1.	Mike Nugent	24	2001–2002 (13)
2.	Vlade Janakievski	15	1979–1980 (5)
3.	Dan Stultz	10	2000 (4)
4.	Vlade Janakievski	10	1978 (8)
5t.	Ryan Pretorius	9	2007 (6)
	Mike Nugent	9	2004 (4)
	Josh Jackson	9	1994–1995 (7)

OHIO STATE

straight from 1979 to 1980. He wore uniform No. 13 and was a two-time All–Big Ten selection.

For more than 20 years, Janakievski has operated the Easy Living Catering and Delicatessen on Lane Avenue in Columbus. He has catered the postgame meal for the Buckeyes for 18 years. Besides the usual deli sandwiches and sides, Easy Living is the place to go for the best feta cheese, kashkaval, olives, and spices.

JUSTIN BOREN
(THE MAN WHO SWITCHED SIDES)

It's 23 miles from Pickerington, Ohio, to Ohio Stadium. Justin Boren took a 399-mile detour en route to the 'Shoe. But once he found it, he was glad he did. Boren was a prep All-America lineman at Pickerington North High School who was recruited by Ohio State and Michigan. His father, Mike, was a linebacker for the Wolverines and led the team in tackles in 1982 and 1983. His mother, Hope, was on the track team at U-M.

When Michigan offered Justin a scholarship, Bo Schembechler called his former star. "He's your son. You tell him where he's going to go." Mike said, "I'm not going to tell him where to go. He has to make this decision for himself." Justin eventually chose Michigan. As a freshman in 2006, he progressed slowly, due to injuries. But by the end of October, he was a starting guard, just the fourth true freshman in U-M history to start on the O-line. The following spring, he was moved to center, and at the conclusion of spring drills, he was listed as the starter. But when backup quarterback Ryan Mallett fumbled two snaps from Boren, the Ohioan

PLAYERS FROM MICHIGAN ON THE
2010 OHIO STATE FOOTBALL ROSTER

OHIO STATE

	Yr.	Pos.	Hometown (H.S.)
Dionte Allen	Jr.	DB	Detroit (St. Mary's)
Reid Fragel	So.	TE	Grosse Pointe Farms (Grosse Pointe South)
Aaron Gant	Sr.	DB	Detroit (St. Mary's)
Johnathan Hankins	Fr.	DL	Dearborn Heights (Southeastern)
James Jackson	So.	WR	Grand Ledge (Grand Ledge)
Taurian Washington	Sr.	WR	Orchard Lake (St. Mary's)

was moved back to guard. Boren alternated between center and guard for the remainder of the year, yet garnered honorable mention All–Big Ten honors.

After the season, head coach Lloyd Carr was replaced by Rich Rodriguez. A week and a half into spring practice, Boren quit. He explained, "Michigan football was a family, built on mutual respect and support for each other from Coach Carr on down. We knew it took the entire family, a team effort, and we all worked together.... I have great trouble accepting that those family values have eroded in just a few months.... That I am unable to perform under these circumstances at the level I expect of myself, and my teammates and Michigan fans deserve, is why I have made the decision to leave."

OHIO STATE

OHIO STATE AWARD-WINNERS

Davey O'Brien Award (Best Quarterback)
Troy Smith   2006

Doak Walker Award (Best Running Back)
Eddie George   1995

Fred Biletnikoff Award (Best Wide Receiver)
Terry Glenn   1995

Rimington Trophy (Best Center)
LeCharles Bentley   2001

Jim Thorpe Award (Best Defensive Back)
Antoine Winfield   1998
Malcolm Jenkins   2008

Butkus Award (Best Linebacker)
Andy Katzenmoyer   1997
James Laurinaitis   2007

Bronko Nagurski Trophy (Top Defensive Player)
James Laurinaitis   2006

Lou Groza Award (Best Kicker)
Mike Nugent   2004

Ray Guy Award (Best Punter)
B.J. Sander   2003

A month later, Boren announced that he would return home and enroll at Ohio State, making him the first player since World War II to transfer from U-M to OSU. Section 14.5.2.B of the Rules of Eligibility in the Big Ten Handbook prohibited Boren from getting a scholarship at one Big Ten school after transferring from another Big Ten school. A week after Justin announced his decision, his younger brother, Zach, committed to OSU, too. Zach said, "Everyone in the whole family is an Ohio State fan now. No one cares about Michigan at all anymore. That was in the past, and we're all looking forward to being Buckeyes and staying Buckeyes for the rest of our lives."

Justin sat out the 2008 season due to transfer rules. He practiced every day, despite not being able to play. In the 2009 season opener, Justin started at left guard, and Zach started at fullback. When the Michigan game finally rolled around, Justin remained quiet, but his former U-M teammates did some talking. Said Michigan lineman David Moosman, "I don't care. He just didn't want to be here. He probably shouldn't have come in the first place. Whose fault was that?" Final score: OSU 21, U-M 10. Following the season, Justin was chosen to the first-team All–Big Ten squad by the Associated Press.

Justin remained quiet prior to the 2010 OSU–U-M game, as well, a 37–7 rout of that school up north. The 2010 season brought more accolades for Justin. He was a second-team All-America pick by the AP and CBS Sports. Not bad for someone who took a while to see what was best for him.

4

TRADITIONS WE LOVE

IT WAS IN THE LATE 18ᵀᴴ CENTURY, before Ohio was officially even a member of the Union, when the term *buckeye* first entered the lexicon as a nickname for a resident of the state. The Native Americans of the region referred to delegate Col. Ebenezer Sproat, at 6′4″ a giant of a man at the time, though probably a little small for the offensive line these days, as *hetuck* (buckeye). Presumably, they were referring to the tree and not the nut. Sproat wore the moniker proudly, and the name spread. A century later, Ohio founded The Ohio State University in Columbus, which quickly adopted the Buckeye as the nickname for its sporting teams (although officially only as of 1950).

Sure, the wood is no good for burning, the bark kind of smells, and the nut is inedible, but the buckeye has one thing going for it that makes it an ideal symbol for Ohio State and its football team: it's incredibly hard to kill. (Much like the beloved traditions of the greatest school and football team in the country.)

"THE BUCKEYE BATTLE CRY"

Get this: this march was written and composed by an Ohio University graduate. On a whim, Frank Crumit is said to have entered a contest for a new Ohio State fight song whose playing by the OSU band would coincide with the opening in 1922 of Ohio Field (now Ohio Stadium). Crumit was a songwriter and vaudeville actor back in the day. The song actually begins with a percussion arrangement certain to send chills up the spines of Buckeyes faithful everywhere. That part of it is known as "The Ramp (Entrance)," and it helps to build a certain fervor for what is to follow. As the rest of the band follows the percussionists onto the field and forms a perfect grid of musicians, the opening strains get everyone on their feet. And then comes the singalong with no less than 105,000 people, regardless of the weather or opponent. And together they sing:

In old Ohio there's a team
That's known throughout the land
Eleven warriors brave and bold
Whose fame will ever stand
And when the ball goes over,
Our cheers will reach the sky
Ohio Field will hear again
The Buckeye Battle Cry!

Drive, drive on down the field
Men of the Scarlet and Gray
Don't let them through that line
We've got to win this game today
COME ON OHIO!
Smash through to victory
We cheer you as you go

THE LOST VERSE

Little known by many OSU fans is the fact that Crumit wrote a second verse for the "Buckeye Battle Cry," which was apparently lost until someone recovered it from a 1924 recording:

> *We'll scatter to the east and west*
> *When college days are done,*
> *And memories will cling around*
> *The dreams of everyone;*
> *We'll play the game of living,*
> *With head and shoulders high!*
> *And where in wear the spirit of*
> *The Buckeye Battle Cry!*

Nice. Very nice, but we don't need it. It's fine with just the first verse, and we'll stick to what we know.

OHIO STATE

Our honor defend
We will fight to the end
for O–HI–O!

"ACROSS THE FIELD"

First recorded by the Criterion Male Quartette and marketed by Gennett Records in 1922, the year Ohio Stadium was built, "Across the Field" was the B side of a 78-RPM record that featured "Football Songs of The Ohio State University." The music was not played by The Best Damned Band in the Land (TBDBITL), but rather by the Gennett Symphony Orchestra.

According to The Ohio State University Marching Band's website, in 1915 OSU student William A. Dougherty Jr. set out to write the perfect fight song for his alma mater. While "Carmen Ohio" was already firmly in place as OSU's school song, Dougherty was of the belief that a song with a peppier tempo was just the ticket for football games and pep rallies. "Across the Field" was—and is—it.

Introduced at a pep rally before the 1915 football game against Illinois and played for the first time at Ohio Field during the same game, the song has become a rallying cry for all Buckeyes teams, despite its football-oriented lyrics. Still, its most popular playings are on fall days at Ohio Stadium during football games (preferably against Michigan). When the Buckeyes are driving toward the opponent's end zone, TBDBITL strikes up the tune

OHIO STATE

"ACROSS THE FIELD" LYRICS

Fight the team across the field
Show them Ohio's here
(We've got the team why don't we)
Set the Earth reverberating
With a mighty cheer
(RAH! RAH! RAH!)
C'mon Ohio!
Hit them hard and see how they fall
Never let that team get the ball
Hail! Hail! The gang's all here
So let's win that old conference now!
(So let's beat that Michigan now!)

According to sgsosu.net, it is unknown when the line, "So let's win that old conference now!" replaced, "So let's beat that Michigan now!"
Admit it, you're feeling the goose bumps, too.

to urge players and fans on to victory, and after every game, the team sings "Across the Field" in the locker room.

"Across the Field" won the President's Cup for the Best University song in the 1916 Ohio State Alumni Association Song Contest. Something of a Grammy. We'll take it.

BUCKEYE LEAVES

The staff at chacha.com can tell us many things. For this book, they told us the *real* story behind Buckeye Leaves. (Leave it to the guy who invented voicemail, Scott Jones, to come up with a solution for quick answers to pressing questions. That's what ChaCha does. Oh, and yes, the capital of Djibouti still is Djibouti.) Anyway, the year actually was 1967—that much of the story we know. The first sticker that Woody Hayes awarded was to Jim Nein, for an interception against Oregon in a 30–0 victory. According to Ohio State lore, the Buckeyes first awarded them in 1968, as they prepared for what ultimately would be "that championship season," Hayes and trainer Ernie Biggs talked about giving players helmet stickers resembling buckeye leaves for outstanding performances in games. Hayes got off and running with the idea, and here we are, still marveling at the sometimes overloaded helmets—except for those hideous, stupid throwback uniforms the Buckeyes were forced to wear in the 2009 and 2010 editions of The Game (no Buckeye Leaves on those helmets, provided as part of a marketing money-grab).

Actually, we believe Woody went one-up on his protégé and 10-year Michigan adversary/nemesis, Bo Schembechler. Here's how that story goes, according to *ESPN College GameDay*,

Ohio State cornerback Anderson Russell holds up his helmet in the midst of his teammates prior to a 2009 game against Penn State in State College, Pennsylvania. The Buckeye Leaf stickers reward big-impact plays and have been an Ohio State football tradition since 1967.

which featured the tradition on its November 27, 2010, broadcast in advance of that day's edition of The Game: helmet stickers first were awarded at Miami of Ohio. Assistant coach Jim Young, later Purdue's head coach, gave stickers to the freshmen team in 1964, and varsity stickers were first awarded by Miami of Ohio head coach Schembechler in 1965, in the shape of tomahawks. Anyone remember those? We thought not. Are Buckeye Leaves known the world over? Let's put it this way: in a men's bathroom in the glittering new shopping mall and airport in Detroit, we noticed one pasted to the inside of a stall door. We Buckeyes leave our marks everywhere—so to speak. But, really, it was an elegant gesture. No conde-scending words scrawled with a Sharpie on the back of that door would have made such a statement bolder. Florida State can have its hideous tomahawk stickers, Clemson it's cartoon-ish tiger-paw stickers, and Georgia those stupid dog biscuit things, but the Buckeye Leaf truly is royalty among paste-ons.

"Woody was always trying to get that extra motivational edge," Rex Kern, OSU's quarterback during that magical fall of the Super Sophs in '68, told John D. Lukacs at espn.com in 2008.

The coach and the trainer thought that outstanding perfor-mances should be rewarded in a tangible way, and that way became the Buckeye Leaf. Time and change will surely show that nothing lasts forever—except for, of course, how firm thy friendship, O–HI–O—and so the leaves grew smaller over the years. The downsized version allows for more to be pasted on the helmets each week.

The Vest liked to award Buckeye Leaves for team perfor-mance, although the stickers themselves have been reduced in size, and the criteria for receiving a Buckeye Leaf has been considerably refined. Coach Jim Tressel favored a teamwork approach over an individual-based award system, according to Lukacs, which means that touchdowns and interceptions no longer necessarily guarantee a coveted sticker. The Vest decided who got what for which big play.

The list of award criteria is so long and so complicated that we've left it out (Michigan followers wouldn't get it). Suffice it to say, if the team does what the coaches game-plan for it to do, Buckeye Leaves all around!

Hayes became parsimonious with regard to handing out the awards. Doling them out suddenly became a big deal, and it was done in a team meeting as opposed to the Vest's quiet decisions based on study of game video.

FYI: one side of the helmet (and it always starts on the left) accommodates up to 40 stickers.

THE VICTORY BELL

It all began after a victory against California on October 2, 1954. As the final gun sounds, and Ohio State has won again, so sounds the 2,420-pound Victory Bell in the southeast tower of Ohio Stadium. Those fine fellows of Alpha Phi Omega fraternity, whose predecessors in the classes of 1943–1945 bestowed the mammoth instrument on the university, do the honors—presumably with earplugs in place for 30 minutes after a victory against that school up north or just 15 minutes for a victory against the pedestrian vanquished. Sweet music, indeed!

MIRROR LAKE

It used to be, but this body of water no longer is naturally occurring. Mirror Lake once was fed by a spring, whose supply was exhausted about 90 years ago, and is now kept full by a Columbus water company.

We've witnessed Ohio State students dripping with Mirror Lake tradition. That is, the intrepid ones hop into the chilly waters the Thursday night (actually, right around midnight) before The Game. It has happened since 1990 as an organized

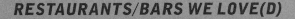

RESTAURANTS/BARS WE LOVE(D)

The Varsity Club
Buckeye Hall of Fame Café
The Agora
The Oar House

OHIO STATE

activity. Prior, it was a few folks who were viewed as goof-balls…until the Buckeyes sent the Wolverines back north with tails neatly tucked "way up there" after OSU victories. So back in 1990 the tradition really got going with the Pride of the Buckeyes, The Best Damn Band in the Land, leading shivering souls on a march to wetness.

The *Lantern*, the critically acclaimed student-run newspaper at Ohio State, tells us that only 100 or so souls were brave enough in 1990 to take a dip, but by 2009, more than 11,000 had either jumped in or stood and cheered the Wet Willies who took the Mirror Lake Plunge.

However, with a change in the Big Ten scheduling to add a bye week in 2010, the Thursday before The Game was, actually, Thanksgiving. No matter. The tradition was moved to Tuesday night, and 6,000 kids still hadn't left for the holiday break—and they participated.

Towel, please?

BUCKEYE GROVE

It's simple: become a first-team All-American, get a tree planted (with a plaque bearing your name at its base) in your honor for your efforts. This tradition got started in 1934—way before the green movement. Nice to know the All-Americans have contributed to battling their carbon footprints since the "dark ages of college football."

When expansion and renovation of Ohio Stadium was complete in 2001, the grove had been moved from the east side of the edifice to the south side. Plantings and ceremonies typically are conducted each spring, just prior to the annual Spring Game, which draws, oh, only about 50,000 to 60,000 fans to the Horseshoe.

SENIOR TACKLE

Begun in 1913 by head coach John Wilce, this is the tradition by which seniors on the team are recognized at the last practice of the season, either before the Michigan game or before departing Columbus to play in a bowl game, and hit the blocking sled one final time.

It used to be a public affair, especially in the Woody Hayes era. Time was, fans could enter Ohio Stadium for free on the Thursday before The Game and watch seniors take a crack at the sled one last time; sometimes the Old Man would stand on the sled to add a bit of weight. Cheerleaders and a smattering of band members would keep the crowd fired up. Now, it's done at the Woody Hayes Athletic Training Facility...in private.

GOLD PANTS

They put their pants on one leg at a time, the same as we do!
—Francis Schmidt, former Ohio State head coach

Before Francis Schmidt had coached his first game for Ohio State, the question of how to beat Michigan was posed to him. The quote accompanying this passage was his response. Damned clever, and a wonderful bit of psychological strategy, too, if we do say so. Schmidt's charges apparently lapped it up. Over the ensuing four editions of The Game, the cumulative score was Ohio State 114, Michigan 0. The coach put together the Gold Pants Club, whose members are awarded a gold charm resembling the Wolverine's gold pants; the award goes to every member of the Buckeyes teams that beat Michigan. It is a cherished award, unless you're a Wolverine or need a tattoo, of course. Bad enough you have to wear gold pants, but to have to see your tormentors wearing them around their necks, yeesh.

BRUTUS BUCKEYE

On October 30, 1965, at the Ohio State homecoming game against Minnesota, a strange critter appeared in Ohio Stadium. Ray Bourhis, a member of Ohio Staters Inc., a student organization, had the idea and solicited help from his fellow OSIs. They fashioned a large buckeye out of papier-mâché, a nut with a huge grin. It was a cumbersome headpiece, and a couple weeks later it was supplanted by a fiberglass replica, and this one included furry eyebrows. According to coach tressel.com: "The rest of the features remained the same. This new nut made its debut at the home game against Iowa, which was also Dad's Day at Ohio State."

The mascot, some five days later, was christened Brutus Buckeye after a campus-wide contest for a name. Kerry Reed, a student, was the winner. The website says the responsibility of caring for Brutus was turned over to Block O, the student spirit organization. That care plan was dismissed by Block O in 1974. The cheerleading program adopted the nut, and one of its own carried the head on his or her shoulders until 1981, when a mascot tryout was initiated. In 1975 they made the head smaller, but fans were less than pleased with the iteration, whose squinting eye and menacing sneer turned off many. It was decided to bring back the predecessor, and all was right with the world. The website reports:

> Another attempt at putting Brutus on a diet fails [in 1977]. The smaller version, which closely resembled the original, might have lost a few inches in size, but put on nearly 60 lbs. in weight! The version retained the happy face, which went to waist level of the performing person, but added a ball cap to rest on top of Brutus' head. The model was well received by fans.

That autumn, Sandy Foreman became the first female to play the role of Brutus, toting the 80-pound version hither and yon.

In 1981 Brutus was put on another diet, this time with a large head that rested on the shoulders of the person chosen to be the mascot. It had a friendlier appearance. Then in 1982 they

Brutus Buckeye, Ohio State's mascot since 1965, leads the marching band onto the field before the 2004 game against Michigan at Ohio Stadium. The Buckeyes won 37–21, naturally. Photo courtesy of Getty Images

changed his appearance again, this time with a "trim figure, sporting a scarlet-and-gray striped shirt with 'Brutus' on the front, and '00' on the back. His pants were scarlet, with the name of his great school embroidered on the sides." Five years later began the nonstop marketing of the nut, whose image was plastered on myriad products. Another makeover? Why not? In 1998, Brutus, looking a bit wan, was given a "tan" so he wouldn't look so tired. And, wouldn't you know it, the next year, Brutus authored his first book, *The Spirit of a Buckeye: Brutus Buckeye's Lessons for Life.*

TUNNEL OF PRIDE

This one is cool, *really* cool. Rex Kern got together with Andy Geiger, the former athletics director at Ohio State, to develop a way to connect the now to the then. Kern, the fabled OSU

OHIO STATE

SKULL SESSION

Okay, let's put it this way: if you consider yourself the consummate Ohio State football fan but you haven't spent time getting pumped up for that day's game by attending the Skull Session, well, maybe you're not so consummate, eh? Having been to hundreds of these—it's part of the tradition, people—we can assure you that the early bird captures the worm on this one. Let's see, Ohio Stadium holds in excess of 105,000 people. St. John Arena, site of the Skull Session holds approximately 10 percent of those people. The point is, get there early and stake your claim to the best seat available. (We like to sit as high as possible on the mezzanine level, and we find the sound to be best from that location.) It's a treat to have "yer innerds" rocked by the fight songs rehearsed with full force. These days, the coach will bring the team through the Skull Session, stopping to say something about it and the game at hand—or let a player do the talking. The place comes unglued. Then the players head out of St. John on a walk south to the 'Shoe. The session starts two hours prior to game time, so plan your pregame experience wisely.

quarterback of the 1968 national champion Buckeyes, thought having a tunnel of humanity, stars of days gone by, greet the current players as they sprinted from the locker room for the kickoff of The Game would be fitting. Geiger helped make it reality. Fitting? It was, and it still is. So in 1994, when Michigan came to town, every former Buckeye in attendance that day was invited down to the field to form the tunnel. We whupped their asses that day 22–6. The tunnel comes out for every home game against the Wolverines, and it also was trotted out for the Notre Dame game in 1995.

"HANG ON SLOOPY"

Union City, Indiana, is a sleepy Ohio border town, but not so sleepy when it comes to Sloopy. Rick and the Raiders, from Union City, recorded the song in 1965. The group's name was changed to The McCoys (to avoid confusion with another popular band of the era, Paul Revere and the Raiders), and their 16-year-old leader, Rick Zehringer, became known as Rick Derringer.

"Hang On Sloopy" is played at every event where The Best Damned Band in the Land performs, and it has been covered by countless rock bands the world over. It also happens to be the official rock song of the state of Ohio.

John Tatgenhorst, who in 1965 was a member of TBDBITL, wrote his own arrangement for the best all-brass band in the world. (He later would become a director of the band.) Tatgenhorst pleaded and cajoled Dr. Charles Spohn, then the director, to allow TBDBITL to play it live at a game. Spohn relented, and against Illinois on October 9 that year, "Sloopy" first was rolled out to a rain-soaked crowd. The following

CAPTAIN'S BREAKFAST

What began in 1934 at Scioto Country Club by Walter Jeffrey of Columbus continues to be a tradition today. Every homecoming weekend, former captains are invited to dine with current captains, each of whom receives a mug emblazoned with his name.

OHIO STATE

OHIO STATE

THE OFFICIAL ROCK SONG OF OHIO

So how did "Hang On Sloopy" become the official rock song of the state? One of the authors' colleagues at the dearly departed *Columbus Citizen-Journal* was columnist Joe Dirck. He was a gifted writer with a quick wit. In April 1985 Dirck read a story about a proposal to make "Louie, Louie" the state rock song of Washington. Dirck decided to write about it. Eventually, the 116th Ohio General Assembly caved in to popular reaction to Dirck's suggestion that "Sloopy" become the official state rock song. A measure was introduced on November 20, 1985, with clauses including:

> WHEREAS, "Hang On Sloopy" is of particular relevance to members of the Baby Boom Generation, who were once dismissed as a bunch of long-haired, crazy kids, but who now are old enough and vote in sufficient numbers to be taken quite seriously.... [and] adoption of this resolution will not take too long, cost the state anything, or affect the quality of life in this state to any appreciable degree, and if we in the legislature just go ahead and pass the darn thing, we can get on with more important stuff.

Well played, Mr. Dirck (and TBDBITL)!

week, in better weather, the band, seated in the stands, played it again, and this time the crowd went wild.

According to the band's website, tbdbitl.osu.edu:

The ability of the song to bring the crowd to its feet has been noted by university officials, particularly in the press box. During the OSU vs. Syracuse game in 1988, Dr. Jon Woods was asked not to play "Sloopy" again until they had time to structurally test the press box. Evidently, there were reports that the press box was shaking. Dr. Paul Droste confirms this rhythmic power, noting that "Sloopy" was used on several occasions to test the structural integrity of the stadium.

When the percussion section goes off to start the song, there's nothing that rivals its riling power over the OSU faithful.

"CARMEN OHIO"

When you get your ass whupped 86–0 at Michigan and have to endure a train ride back to Columbus, you had best find ways to occupy your time. For Fred Cornell, a freshman player on the 1902 Buckeyes, the solution was to come up with the university's alma mater. The website sgsosu.net notes Cornell was a member of a local church choir and a member of the Beta Theta Pi men's glee club. (He also wound up starting on the OSU basketball and baseball teams, and set a school record in the high hurdles.)

What began as jotting some notes on an envelope morphed into a full songwriting experience. Reports sgsosu.net:

> He used some lines from a Yale song that he knew and set his lines to the melody of the hymn, "Spanish Chant." The word *carmen* means "song or poem" in Spanish. He completed the song over the next few months and performed it

The Ohio State Buckeyes Marching Band, also known as The Best Damn Band in the Land (TBDBITL for short), takes the field at Ohio Stadium during halftime of the Bucks' 31–6 thumping of the Iowa Hawkeyes on September 24, 2005.
Photo courtesy of Getty Images

publicly for the first time in December 1903 for Ohio governor Judson Harmon. The song was shelved until a group of students sang it at a bonfire in 1906. The words and music were included in the Ohio State–Michigan football game program later that year, and "Carmen Ohio" has been sung at every home football game since.

Cornell died in 1969 at the age of 87 after a successful career in the auto industry and shipbuilding. Today, the words to "Carmen Ohio" are etched in a granite slab near the Orton bell tower on the southwest corner of the Oval.

OHIO STATE

THE LYRICS TO "CARMEN OHIO"

Oh! Come let's sing Ohio's praise,
And songs to Alma Mater raise;
While our hearts rebounding thrill,
With joy which death alone can still.
Summer's heat and Winter's cold,
The seasons pass, the years will roll;
Time and change will surely show
How firm thy friendship—O–HI–O.

(These days, they cut it off there, but for those who are compelled to finish it, sing on.)

These jolly days of priceless worth,
By far the gladdest days of earth,
Soon will pass and we not know
How dearly we love Ohio.
We should strive to keep they name
Of fair repute and spotless fame;
So, in college halls we'll grow
To love thee better—O–HI–O.

Though age may dim our mem'ry's store,
We'll think of happy days of yore,
True to friend and frank to foe,
As sturdy sons of O hi o.
If on seas of care we roll,
'Neath blackened sky, or barren shoal,
Thoughts of thee bid darkness go,
Dear Alma Mater—O–HI–O.

Or, if you can't memorize them, the massive south end zone scoreboard scrolls them during the pregame festivities and then again when the coaches and the team, arm in arm and swaying to the beat, sing along with the band, which is situated in the lower level of the south stands. If that scene doesn't raise goose bumps, send chills up or down your spine (you choose the direction), and/or put a lump in your throat, well, you just don't have Scarlet and Gray coursing through your being. It also means you're probably from Michigan. And a complete loser.

SCRIPT *Ohio*

This is where we, the authors, come in, because, as we noted at the beginning of this volume, we're a virtual lock to dot the *i* in this formation. Or not. Regardless, is there any introduction anywhere in the annals of college marching bands that can top this? "And now, the most memorable tradition in college band history, the Incomparable *Script Ohio!*" If you answered yes, you're probably from Michigan (and all that that entails).

Anyway, with those very words begin the opening notes of "Le Règiment de Sambre et Meuse," a French march to which the precision footwork of the 192-member band is set in motion. From a block O formation three layers deep and in single-file, the drum major leads his band into a formation spelling *Ohio* in, yup, script. They've been pulling this duty since 1936. When the last *o* is formed, the drum major prances out to the top of the *i*, followed usually by a senior Sousaphone player, who becomes the dot. TBDBITL tells us sometimes, not often, they have had a celebrity, like Bob Hope, Woody Hayes, OSU president Novice Fawcett and his wife, retired ticket

The Best Damn Band in the Land spells out Ohio *in script, with the Sousaphone player dotting the* i, *before the 2004 Michigan game at Ohio Stadium, a tradition dating back to 1936.* Photo courtesy of Getty Images

director Robert Ries, and Jack Nicklaus dot the *i*. OSU president Gordon Gee, his wife, retired directors Dr. Paul Droste, Jack Evans, their wives, and heavyweight champion Buster Douglas also have dotted the *i* with the OSU Alumni Band. In addition, all 13 seniors of the 2002–2003 national championship football team dotted the *i* at the national championship celebration. The most recent honorary *i*-dot was performed during the Alumni Reunion Game on September 5, 2009, by Senator John Glenn and his wife, Annie.

As for your intrepid authors, it's simply a matter of time before TBDBITL caves and gives us our chance. (By the way, *i*-dotting is not for sale. We know this because we asked. *Apparently*, $47.39 was not enough. No matter. We are, if nothing else, undaunted.)

OHIO STATE

OSU ALUMNI WE LOVE

James Thurber, R.L. Stine, and **Cynthia Ozick,** authors
Roy Lichtenstein, artist
Richard Lewis, comedian
Dwight Yoakam, country singer
Patricia Heaton, actress (*Everybody Loves Raymond*)
Barbara Reynolds, nationally syndicated columnist
Jack Buck, sports announcer
Clark Kellogg, CBS Sports
Jesse Owens, Ford Konno, Bob Clotworthy, and **Glenn Davis,**
    Olympic athletes
Jack Nicklaus, golfer
Bobby Knight, basketball coach
John Havlicek and **Jerry Lucas,** basketball players
George Steinbrenner, owner, N.Y. Yankees
Frank Howard, baseball player
Alice "Lefty" Hohlmayer, original member of the All
    American Girls Professional Baseball League
Charles Bassett, Nancy Currie, and **Robert H. Lawrence Jr.,**
    astronauts
Larry Sanger, Wikipedia cofounder
Paul Flory (chemistry) and **William A. Fowler** (physics),
    Nobel Laureates

5

STORIES WE LOVE

There are so many anecdotes from the history of The Game that we decided to limit the ones we love to a top five. So, in David Letterman style, here we go.

NO. 5

It was the 81st edition of The Game, November 17, 1984, and while the name Earle Bruce will never be uttered in the same sentence as "offensive mastermind" (well, except for this one), this was one of those exceptions. The game was played in Columbus, and the Buckeyes had already lost, uncharacteristically, two games that season, one each to Purdue and Wisconsin. It was nearly unthinkable, what with a roster stocked with eventual All-Pros Pepper Johnson, Cris Carter, and Jim Lachey, as well as Mike Lanese and Keith Byars, to name but a few, but the notion of underperforming was floating around Columbus, Lanese told us for *The Game of My Life*. Still and all, OSU was in the running for an outright Big Ten championship. Could it happen? We'll see. To earn that title and the ensuing bid to the Rose Bowl—OSU had not been since Earle Bruce's first season, 1979—all the Buckeyes had to do was vanquish Michigan, 6–4 entering The Game. Bruce put together a different game plan, one that had quarterback Mike Tomczak actually running the option. Enter Lanese: with the clock closing in on halftime and the Bucks up 7–0, Lanese, who had never returned a punt for a touchdown and never fumbled, decided against a fair catch. He made a couple moves and...fumbled. Michigan closed to within 7–3. In the second half, the Wolverines made it 7–6. Enter Lanese again: on a third-and-12 play, which the Buckeyes needed to convert to keep the Michigan defense on the field, Lanese ran an in route, but he overran it...and here came the pass from T-czak. In a split second, Lanese considerably lengthened his arms somehow and caught what would be a game-changing, 17-yard pass for a first down. The Buckeyes would score on that drive and add another touchdown later, and they ended up winning 21–6.

NO. 4

Michigan, everybody's No. 1 at the time, came strutting into Ohio Stadium on November 25, 1972, expecting a victory. The Buckeyes were underdogs in their own house. How often does *that* happen? They shouldn't have been underdogs. Period. That afternoon, an upset of mammoth proportions took place when OSU slammed the door on Michigan's conference title dreams, winning 14–11 with drama often played out in The Game. The Buckeyes had three unbelievable goal-line stands against the Wolverines' high-octane offense. The Buckeyes offense had scored more points than any other team had against Michigan, which gave up an average of five points a game that season. Defense carried the day for the Buckeyes, rising up and snuffing out nearly every Michigan challenge. After the game, as OSU was celebrating it's conference-title clinch and trip to the Rose Bowl, someone hollered at Coach

BUCKEYES BOOKS WE LOVE

I REMEMBER WOODY

OHIO STATE '68: ALL THE WAY TO THE TOP

GAME CHANGERS: THE GREATEST PLAYS
IN OHIO STATE FOOTBALL HISTORY

THE OFFICIAL OHIO STATE
FOOTBALL ENCYCLOPEDIA

WHAT IT MEANS TO BE A BUCKEYE

GREATEST MOMENTS IN OHIO STATE HISTORY

WOODY HAYES AND THE 100-YARD WAR

GLORY YEARS

THE GAME OF MY LIFE

Woody Hayes that the president was on the phone. "Which president?" he asked. "Nixon," someone responded. "Tell him he'll have to wait; I'm talking to my men." Nixon understood, for he and Woody were friends.

NO. 3

This one could be considered the epitome of the Ten-Year War between Hayes and his pupil (and former assistant coach) Bo Schembechler. It was November 21, 1970, and both teams were undefeated and untied entering the game. The Super Sophs had become the Sensational Seniors. This would be the rubber match, of sorts, for that class. The year before (must we relive that excruciating afternoon in Michigan Stadium in Bo's rookie stint with them? we must…for a second) the Wolverines pulled off one of the greatest upsets in The Game, a 24–12 shocker. For this game, though, Hayes had his players hyper-prepared. Actually, the prep work began with the manufacturing of a rug on which everyone associated with the Ohio State program would walk going to and coming from the practice field at the then North Facility. In its fibers was woven the score of that game up north the previous season. There was no forgetting. This was the culmination of a year's worth of work to cast aside the dastardly demons. And that's exactly what OSU did. Without getting into the Xs and Os of the afternoon, offensive tackle John Hicks perhaps put it best: "We beat 'em up pretty good. We manhandled them." Final score: OSU 20, Michigan 9. "We wanted it more than Michigan…for nearly a whole year. And the really great thing was, all we did was [study] the plan and execute it."

NO. 2

Sorry, fans, this anecdote is worth reading, even though we got screwed out of an improbable victory up at Ann Arbor in 1971, when we probably didn't even belong in the same "house" with those guys. Although we lost 10–7, the run-up to the game featured Hayes at his best. His defensive coordinator, George Hill, was in his first season, having joined the staff from Duke. One night the week of The Game, Hill told us, he got a phone call from Hayes. The Old Man was looking at "pictures, that's what he called film. Pictures." And he had a lot on his mind at 1:00 AM. Hill snapped out of his slumber and was at full attention.

"How in the hell are we going to stop that backfield of [Ed] Shuttlesworth, Billy Taylor, and [Glenn] Doughty and that bunch?" Hayes asked his assistant.

Hill told his boss, "Coach, I've faced a lot better backfield than that."

To which Hayes inquired, "What do you mean, you've faced a better backfield than that?"

"Yeah," said Hill, "last season when I was at Duke, coaching against you, I had to find a way to stop [John] Brockington, [Larry] Zelina, [Leophus] Hayden, and [Rex] Kern. That was a helluva lot better backfield than Michigan's is."

"You're goddamned right it was," replied Coach Hayes. "We'll be all right then, won't we?"

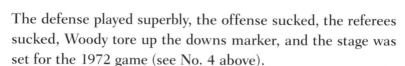

The defense played superbly, the offense sucked, the referees sucked, Woody tore up the downs marker, and the stage was set for the 1972 game (see No. 4 above).

NO. 1

This one is the all-timer for us. Never mind that Ohio State had just beaten Michigan to advance to the Tostitos BCS National Championship Game against Miami. It's what happened in the aftermath of the November 23, 2002, game that still has us goose-bumping. Understand, this regular season closer was a do-or-(sort of)-die game for the Buckeyes. Ohio State had been teetering on disaster the previous two games, a late victory at Purdue and an overtime triumph against Illinois. Now, here comes the school up north, 9–2 against our 12–0, with absolutely nothing to lose. An ardent supporter of the Buckeyes was so incredibly uptight beforehand that we saw him vomit in the parking lot, just west of the press box elevator. Said our buddy, gameface restored: "There. I'm ready. We've got this one!"

We had every reason to be on edge as the game neared; they had screwed us out of undefeated seasons in 1993, 1995, and 1996. It couldn't happen again, not with Jim Tressel at the reins, could it? We trailed 9–7 at halftime, but there was no sense of impending doom. Holding Michigan to three field goals was something of a comfort moment, but then dawned the fourth quarter. We got the ball at the Michigan 43, and quarterback Craig Krenzel, one play after sneaking for a first down, passed to tailback Maurice Clarett, who took the ball to the Michigan 6. Okay, this is what we love about Buckeyes fans: you'd have thought each had won a $225 million

Freshman tailback Maurice Clarett's fourth-quarter catch down to the Michigan 6-yard-line set up the go-ahead touchdown in Ohio State's 14–9 win to continue the Buckeyes' perfect 2002 season. Clarett finished the game with 119 rushing yards and a TD. Photo courtesy of Getty Images

Powerball play. The celebration was underway—and OSU was trailing 9–7. Oh, about that pass play? Austin Murphy, the superlative writer for *Sports Illustrated*, did some digging after the game and discovered its name, something every Buckeyes fan should commit to memory: Gun Switch Right Dart 59 X Skinny Wheel. That meant Clarett was to swoop out of the backfield as the wideout ran a post pattern down the field to occupy/confuse the secondary of Michigan. The ball went to

Clarett, and two plays later OSU was up 14–9, courtesy of Maurice Hall's three-yard dash to the end zone. What a drive, what a play, what a crowd! All hell, indeed, was breaking loose all the way up to C Deck.

Ultimately, the Buckeyes would prevail as Will Allen intercepted a John Navarre pass in the end zone with one second remaining. Tostitos, anyone? This is what makes this story the most memorable: a mass of humanity on the field, Buckeyes pumping their helmets high, players throwing wristbands and headbands to fans, and above it all…with Woody Hayes smiling, Krenzel, looking as delirious as the fans on the field, was bodysurfed across the field by his adoring public. That is a scene we hope to see again.

6

COACHES WE LOVE

FROM HUMBLE BEGINNING ROSE a proud legacy of coaching. Never mind that Alexander S. Lilley (1890–1891) won three and lost five, or his successor, Jack Ryder (1892–1895, 1898), OSU's first paid coach at $150 a season, went 22–22–2, or that the next guy, Charles A. Hickey (1896) kept OSU mired in mediocrity at 5–5–1. It really got going when, after David Edwards laid a 1–7–1 egg in 1897, John B. Eckstorm (1899–1901) reeled off a 22–4–3 record in three seasons.

Eckstorm was the true sparkmaster, the first winning coach in school history. He lit the fuse that ultimately would ignite a wide swath across the college football landscape, allowing the Buckeyes to become a perennial national power.

When, for unknown reasons, Eckstorm stepped down after the 1901 season, Perry Hale (1902–1903, 14–5–2), E.R. Sweetland (1904–1905, 14–7–2), A.E. Hernstein (1906–1909, 28–10–1), and Howard Jones (1910, 6–1–3) held down the fort. (Jones, incidentally, would go on to have a stellar career in coaching at Iowa and USC, and he was inducted into the College Football Hall of Fame.) Next came Harry Vaughn (1911, 5–3–2) and John R. Richards (1912, 6–3–0) before John W. Wilce (1913–1928) came to town and reeled off a 78–33–9 record.

It was Wilce who so stirred fanaticism with Ohio State football that the Buckeyes were known to nearly everyone nationwide. He would coach the first Ohio State All-American, Boyd Cherry (along with 14 others), and OSU's first true star, Chic Harley. It didn't hurt that he also won three conference championships. Wilce resigned in 1928 to practice medicine. The OSU fight song "Across the Field" (detailed in chapter 4, "Traditions We Love") was written as a tribute to Wilce.

So in comes Sam S. Willaman (1929–1933, 26–10–5) to keep things interesting before OSU's next superstar coach, Francis A. Schmidt, took the helm, which he held from 1934 to 1940. He had a respectable 39–16–1 record (RichRod would have given *anything* for a mark like that, eh?).

At any rate, Schmidt had the unenviable task of succeeding the wildly popular Willaman. He brought with him a new offense that contained many trick plays and was called "razzle dazzle" by the press. He may be most famous for his comment in reference to OSU's troubles with U-M before the Michigan game in 1934: "They put their pants on one leg at a time same as we do!" The team went on to beat U-M after that comment, and the Gold Pants Club was invented to give a miniature pair of gold pants to any player who contributed in a defeat of Michigan. Schmidt resigned in 1940, giving rise to the Paul

Ohio State head football coach Francis A. Schmidt, pictured in 1934, helped turn around the Buckeyes' misfortunes against the school up north by reminding his players, "They put their pants on one leg at a time same as we do!"

Brown Era (okay, really just three seasons). He went 18–8–1 with the Buckeyes, but later in life was often considered to be a legend of the game. Cool fact: Brown very badly wanted to play football for OSU, but he was considered too small, and the Buckeyes would not give him a uniform. Instead, he went to Miami of Ohio, but his love for OSU never stopped. He started his prolific coaching career at Massillon, where he was 80–8–2 in nine seasons, including a stretch when he went 58–1–1. Brown then went to Columbus, where, in 1942, under his leadership, OSU won its first national football championship. A legend was furthered. It is roundly recognized that, as

WOODY HAYES QUOTES WE LOVE

"There's nothing that cleanses your soul like getting the hell kicked out of you."

"Son, women give birth to babies every day of the year, but we will only once play this game against SMU."

"I've had smarter people around me all my life, but I haven't run into one yet that can outwork me."

"If we worked half as hard as our band, we'd be champions."

"We had a secret agreement among ourselves that anyone who mentioned roses would get a punch in the nose—unless it was a lady over 80."

"Balanced offense? That's a bunch of unadulterated bullshit."

"If those SOBs want to fight the Civil War all over again, we'll certainly do it." (Pregame speech, 1978 Gator Bowl vs. Clemson)

"Sure, marijuana will help 'em graduate—graduate to cocaine!"

"The minute I think I'm getting mellow, I'm retiring. Who ever heard of a mellow winner?"

would be the case with one of his successors, Woody Hayes, Brown carried a true hatred for losing, especially to that team from up north. Right on, PB!

After Brown flew the coop, Carroll C. Widdoes (1944–1945, 16–2) had an undefeated season and a No. 2 national ranking. Get this: he moved aside following his second season at the Buckeyes helm after the 1945 season, making a decision we don't quite understand. He swapped posts with Paul Bixler, who had been the offensive coordinator. Huh? Bixler lasted one strange 4–3–2 season before the university brought in Wes Fesler, a "Buckeye guy." The former standout end and fullback for OSU hung around for four seasons, through 1950, and had a semi-respectable 21–13–3 mark; that included, though, a Big Ten championship and a Rose Bowl. Wesley is one of the greatest figures in OSU football history. Fesler resigned, though, in 1950, citing tremendous pressure to win in Columbus.

And so the table was set for the modern-era dominance to be orchestrated by one Wayne Woodrow "Woody" Hayes. Taking over in 1951 after coaching at Denison University and Miami of Ohio, Hayes toiled tirelessly through his 1978 firing, and he won 205 games, lost 61, and tied 10. In truth, we could fill a book with Woody's accomplishments and what folks have to say about him. (Actually, we did: *I Remember Woody*. Read it, it's good for you—and we love royalties!)

Nonetheless, we're overly fond of the man who brought the Buckeyes national championships in 1954, 1957, 1968, and 1970, as well as 13 Big Ten Conference championships (1954–1955, 1957, 1961, 1968–1970, 1972–1977). Tenacious, studious, hard-working, and as diligent as they come, he expected the same of his players and others associated with the program.

He was fired after the 1978 Gator Bowl, during which he threw a punch at Clemson linebacker Charlie Bauman. The player had intercepted an Art Schlichter pass and had the temerity to taunt the OSU sideline. That proved too much for Hayes, a defender of his troops to the end. Out came the fist and out went his job. We're hopeful history will not judge Hayes on that misstep.

So who wants to follow a guy who probably could have won his party's nomination for governor? How about one of his former players and a former assistant? Earle Bruce, from 1979 to his firing in 1987, compiled a record of 81 victories, 26 losses, and one tie. He won 75 percent of his games, but he came to be known as "ol' 9-and-3 Earle." Most colleges and universities would canonize a coach for averaging 9–3 each season, but not OSU. He was fired the week of The Game at Ann Arbor. He had the last laugh, though, winning the game, ending up with a winning record against the Wolverines, and to show he was truly a gentleman, wore a suit and a fedora to his final game as OSU coach.

Meanwhile, out at Arizona State was a guy who had just won the Rose Bowl—and at the university they really like Rose Bowl winners. Buckeye Nation, meet John Cooper. The year was 1988 (he would last until 2001 with a record of 111–43–4), and some rebuilding was in order. Cooper did it, bringing in top talent, but it never really translated. Every time the Buckeyes had a lofty national ranking, some team or another knocked them on their asses. Cooper's good-ol'-boy act was

QUOTES ᴏɴ WOODY HAYES WE LOVE

"If I had to go into a battle and I needed someone loyal and courageous to cover my blindside, I know damn well Woody would be my man. I know, too, that God hasn't created a more generous, compassionate, or more understanding man than Woody Hayes."

—Jack Tatum

"When you play for Woody, you need all the faith you can get."

—Cornelius Greene on why he read the Bible so much

"You were afraid of him as a freshman, you hated him as a sophomore, you liked him as a junior, and you loved him as a senior."

—Tom Skladany

"Though his tenure at Ohio State spanned the turbulent years of the Civil Rights Movement, the only colors that ever mattered to Hayes were OSU's scarlet and gray; black and white were irrelevant."

—*Columbus Dispatch* sports editor Paul Hornung

"The man is insufferable in victory, indomitable in defeat."

—Big Ten commissioner Bill Reed

"Woody is a God-fearing man. It's nice to know he's afraid of somebody."

—Archie Griffin

starting to wear thin, too (not with us—we found him to be mostly a good coach) in Columbus and elsewhere. His undoing, though, was a 2–10–1 record against that school up north. Too much for the university to bear, he was sent packing.

Enter Jim Tressel, the Senator, the Vest, the Governor, or anything else he's been nicknamed. We gotta tell you, even though he had been an assistant on OSU teams previously, we scratched our heads over his hiring. From Youngstown State? Really? Really. Okay, let's see how this goes.

Well, the first thing he did was to announce at an OSU basketball game that his lone goal at that moment was to kick Michigan's ass. We were loving that big time.

He had a bumpy beginning, playing with Cooper's leftovers in a new system, and he finished 7–5. However, he did beat Michigan, and all was right with the world. The next season: national championship! Nobody was arguing then. Tressel, perhaps unfairly, was considered a mostly conservative coach. That may well have been the case on some occasions, but on others he was way out there with an attack plan that confounded the opponent. The man could recruit, too, finishing easily in the top 10 each year with most rating services.

With their 22nd head football coach, OSU played in three BCS National Championship Games. That 2002 squad recorded the first 14–0 season record in major college football since Penn went 15–0 in 1897. After resigning following the end of the 2010 season, Tressel's OSU record stood at 106–22, including seven Big Ten titles; a 6–4 bowl record; a 5–3 record in BCS bowl games, and an otherworldly 9–1 record against the school up north. Only Hayes, with 16, had more OSU victories against Michigan.

With that in mind, here, then, is a closer look at the Ohio State coaches we love.

WOODY HAYES

All of you know the basics of Wayne Woodrow Hayes' football career: head coach at Denison (1946–1948), Miami of Ohio (1949–1950), and Ohio State (1951–1978). A lifetime record of 238–72–10 overall, including a mark of 205–61–10 at Ohio State with four national championships and 13 Big Ten Conference titles.

Perhaps our favorite Woody story emanates from a disputed 16–13 loss at Michigan State in 1974. In 1974 Ohio State was ranked No. 1 in the nation entering the game at East Lansing. The Buckeyes had the ball at the goal line in the waning seconds. Fullback Champ Henson, one of Woody's all-time favorites, took the ball and appeared to be across the plane. The referees gathered and, looking more like the Keystone Kops, decided, in fact, Henson had *not* scored a touchdown. Actually, he had, and had there been instant replay at that time, it would have been confirmed. So the officials tucked tail and raced into the referees' room in the nearby Kellogg Center, not so much fearing backlash from any Buckeyes supporters in the crowd but more likely from Hayes alone.

In the OSU locker room, Hayes went off on something of a 10-megaton volcanic eruption. When he was reminded to calm down, given his heart attack of earlier in the year, Hayes,

Woody Hayes was much more than a coach to his players. To alumni and fans, he represented Ohio State and brought the Buckeyes football program to a prominence it has never relinquished.

taking his vial of heart medication in his hand, screamed, "Fuck my heart!" He tossed the bottle on the floor and stomped on it. Moments later, he turned to his team, still enraged, and shouted, "You motherfuckers like to fight, don't you? Let's go kick their asses!" The players lined up single file behind the Old Man. He was the first out the door, on the way to the

MSU locker room, when he encountered the commissioner of the Big Ten, Wayne Duke. Poor Duke, he probably had major shrinkage going on as Hayes approached him. There were no pleasantries exchanged. Woody, something of a raging bull at that moment, headed straight for the bewildered commissioner, slammed him up against the wall, and, damn any consequences for what was about to unfold, commanded Duke to "tell my team they got fucked."

Duke stammered, "Woody, they got fucked."

And Woody followed with, "All right, fellas, let's get on the bus."

The Buckeyes went to the bus outside the stadium. Before they were about to leave, a group of Spartans fans stood in front of the bus, playing the dangerous role of a heckling crowd. Hayes told the driver, "Fuck 'em. Run 'em over." Finally, the bus left the parking lot. Without further incident, we might add.

Hayes was way more than a football coach. He was a lover of all history (especially military history), great literature, politics, and helping people who needed it most (although he loathed any notion that others knew that about him). In all the world, there was only one.

But what makes Woody Hayes the greatest ever was how he cared for his student-athletes. "You *will* graduate from The Ohio State University," he told every recruit, and then did everything in his immense power to make it happen. He cared for the young men and women in the armed forces, cared for the sick and needy, and cared for the people of Ohio.

OHIO STATE

WOODY THE MOTIVATOR

Woody Hayes was the master at motivating his troops. Some of his most common methods of showing his displeasure were to tear his block O baseball cap to smithereens, stomp on his trademark glasses, or rip his Ohio State University Athletic Department T-shirt to shreds. But were some of Woody's outbursts premeditated?

Jimmy Moore was a Buckeyes tight end from 1975 to 1978, who played for the Baltimore Colts in the NFL. He recalled Woody's temper:

> I saw him get mad all the time, but it wasn't malicious. He would scream and holler and tear his T-shirts and break his glasses. He called me into his office one day, and we were talking about something, and he realized his desk drawer was open. He slammed it shut. Really quickly, I mean. I saw what was in that drawer! He must've had 20 pairs of eyeglasses in that drawer! You know, the ones he was always breaking when he got mad? He liked to play those psychological games. Boz [equipment manager and co-conspirator John Bozick] used to cut Woody's T-shirts so they'd be easy to tear if he got angry. And the back of his hats, too!

So, did Bozick cut Woody's caps and T-shirts?

"That's not true," Bozick claimed. "That's just not true. None of them was ever cut. In the old days, every baseball cap was very, very susceptible to being torn, so consequently, he could tear them. As time went on and we switched caps, he'd step on them and jump on them a bit, because he couldn't tear them apart. But I guess it made for a good story."

JIM TRESSEL

Bill Gates' team of software engineers couldn't have devised a seemingly more appropriate head coach for Ohio State than Jim Tressel. Consider: Tressel grew up in Mentor, Ohio, and was a star quarterback, the son of a football coach who had attended Ohio State. Tressel played for his father at Baldwin-Wallace College in Berea, Ohio, and earned four varsity letters while being named all-conference as a senior. He then became a football coach, working as an assistant at Akron, Miami of Ohio, and Syracuse. In 1983 he became the quarterbacks and receivers coach at Ohio State.

After three seasons as a Buckeyes assistant, he was named the head coach at Youngstown State. There, Tressel compiled a record of 135–57–2 from 1986 to 2000, winning four NCAA Division I-AA national championships.

In 2001 Tressel was named the head coach at Ohio State, a position he was groomed for his entire life. In his 10 seasons leading the Buckeyes, he was 106–22. During his tenure, OSU was 66–14 in the Big Ten with seven Big Ten titles, one national championship, and two national runner-up finishes.

Tressel also is involved with local and national charities, including the Fellowship of Christian Athletes, Athletes in Action, the James Cancer Center of the Ohio State University Medical Center, the OSU Libraries, and multiple NCAA inquiries.

PAUL BROWN

Paul Brown was a quarterback at Washington High School in Massillon who enrolled at Ohio State in 1925. After a season of

OHIO STATE

OSU NATIONAL CHAMPIONSHIPS (7)

Year	Record	Coach
1942	9–1	Paul Brown
1954	10–0	Woody Hayes
1957	9–1	Woody Hayes
1961	8–0–1	Woody Hayes
1968	10–0	Woody Hayes
1970	9–1	Woody Hayes
2002	14–0	Jim Tressel

taking the pounding of big-time college football, Brown transferred to Miami of Ohio, where he earned all-conference honors.

He excelled in the classroom, qualifying for a Rhodes Scholarship, but with the coming of the Great Depression, he passed on the chance for advanced academic work. Instead, he became a high school football coach in Maryland. After two seasons on the East Coast and a quick stint in law school, Brown returned to Ohio to become the head coach of his hometown high school team. In nine seasons at Massillon Washington High School, his teams were 80–8–2, including a 35-game winning streak.

Brown was named head coach at Ohio State prior to the 1941 season. His first season, the Buckeyes were 6–1–1, finished second in the conference, and were No. 13 in the AP poll.

The following year, the Buckeyes won the national championship with a 9–1 record. The team used just three seniors, along with 16 juniors and 24 sophomores (including Les Horvath). World War II recruitment decimated the Buckeyes team, and in 1943 OSU fell to 3–6.

Brown himself was inducted into the U.S. Navy in 1944. While serving, he was head coach of the Great Lakes Naval Station football team. His Bluejackets squad went 15–5–2 over two years. Following the war, like many of his former players, Brown didn't return to Columbus. He opted to take a position with the new Cleveland team in the All-America Football Conference as part-owner, vice president, general manager, and head coach. So popular was Brown that, in a poll of the team's fans, the nickname "Browns" was selected.

As a pro coach, Brown was 206–104–10 with seven league titles in 25 years (Cleveland 1946–1962 and Cincinnati 1968–1975). Brown was known as an innovator and influencer. Among the coaches who either played for him or coached under him were Don Shula, Bill Walsh, Lou Saban, Weeb Ewbank, Otto Graham, Chuck Noll, Ara Parseghian, Blanton Collier, Sid Gillman, Abe Gibron, Bruce Coslet, and Sam Wyche.

One little-known item about Brown is that he wanted to return to Ohio State as its head football coach in 1951. However, Brown had disturbed many of the Buckeyes fans by not returning to Columbus following the war and by signing many Ohio State players to professional contracts before their college eligibility had expired (as was allowed following the war). He had an official job interview with school officials, but the university board rejected Brown and instead chose Woody Hayes.

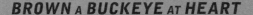

OHIO STATE

BROWN A *BUCKEYE* AT *HEART*

All one has to do to realize the importance of Paul Brown is to remember that he had an NFL team named after him (the Cleveland Browns), which is an honor no one else has ever or will ever be able to claim. But Brown was always a Buckeye at heart. Before his death in 1991, Brown wrote, "My first two years at Ohio State were the happiest, most exciting, and most rewarding period of my life, better in some respect than the years in Cleveland, because coaching the Buckeyes had been my ultimate dream." The importance of Paul Brown to football is immeasurable, and OSU fans should be honored to call this football legend a Buckeye.

EARLE BRUCE

Earle Bruce grew up wanting to be an Ohio State football hero. He was a fullback on the Buckeyes' freshman team in 1950, but a knee injury prior to the 1951 season ended his playing career. Bruce left school and headed home, but rookie Ohio State coach Woody Hayes saw something in Bruce. Hayes summoned Bruce back to campus and added him to the coaching staff.

Following his graduation from Ohio State in 1953, Bruce embarked on a high school coaching career. As a head coach at Salem, Sandusky, and Massillon high schools in Ohio, Bruce's teams were a combined 82–12–3 over 10 seasons.

That success enabled Bruce to return to Columbus as a Buckeyes assistant coach. But after years under Hayes, Bruce took the head job at the University of Tampa. After one season

OHIO STATE COACHES *IN THE* PRO FOOTBALL HALL OF FAME

	OSU Years	Pro Team(s)
Paul Brown	1941–1943	Cleveland Browns
Sid Gillman	1931–33 (end),	Los Angeles Rams,
	1938–40 (asst. coach)	San Diego Chargers, and
		Houston Oilers

OHIO STATE

at Tampa (where Bruce was 10–2 with a win in the Tangerine Bowl), Bruce was named head coach at Iowa State. From 1973 to 1978, the Cyclones were 36–32 with two bowl game appearances.

In 1979 Bruce was named to succeed his mentor, Woody Hayes, as head coach of the Buckeyes. Bruce's first team finished 8–0 in the Big Ten and 11–1 overall with the only loss in the season-ending Rose Bowl.

The next six seasons the Buckeyes wound up 9–3. The Buckeyes finished 10–3 in 1986, then 6–4–1 in 1987. Bruce was informed he would not return as the Buckeyes' head coach prior to The Game in 1987.

In nine seasons at Ohio State, the Buckeyes were 81–26–1, including 57–17 in the Big Ten. The Buckeyes won or shared four Big Ten titles and were 5–3 in bowl games. The team finished among the top 15 in the final AP poll eight times and in

Earle Bruce is lifted up on the shoulders of his players after leading Ohio State past Michigan 23–20 in Ann Arbor on November 21, 1987, just days after he was fired. He spent nine years as the Buckeyes' head coach.

the top 10 three times. Perhaps most important of all, Bruce went 5–4 against that school up north.

But it wasn't good enough—not for an Ohio State following that had grown accustomed to national championships and

Rose Bowls, not appearances in the Liberty, Holiday, and Citrus bowls.

Today, Bruce is one of the most popular former coaches. He is an analyst for Buckeyes games and a frequent speaker on the charity circuit.

FRANCIS SCHMIDT

If anyone gets credit for making Ohio State into a formidable foe for Michigan and the rest of the Big Ten Conference, Francis Schmidt should be on the short list. It was Schmidt who reversed the Buckeyes' fortunes against the Wolverines by leading the Buckeyes to three consecutive shutout wins over Michigan in the 1930s.

OSU COACHES IN THE COLLEGE FOOTBALL HALL OF FAME

	Coached	Record	Inducted
Howard Jones	1910	6–1–3	1951
John Wilce	1913–1928	78–33–9	1954
Francis Schmidt	1934–1940	39–16–1	1971
Woody Hayes	1951–1978	205–61–10	1983
Earle Bruce	1979–1987	81–26–1	2002
John Cooper	1988–2000	111–43–4	2008

OHIO STATE

OHIO STATE

CONFERENCE CHAMPIONSHIPS (37)

Ohio Athletic Conference (OAC)

1906 (Albert E. Herrnstein)

1912 (John Richards)

Big Ten

1916, 1917, 1920 (John Wilce, 3)

1935, 1939 (Francis Schmidt, 2)

1942 (Paul Brown)

1944 (Carroll Widdoes)

1949 (Wes Fesler)

1954, 1955, 1957, 1961, 1968–1970, 1972–1977
(Woody Hayes, 13)

1979, 1981, 1984, 1986 (Earle Bruce, 4)

1993, 1996, 1998 (John Cooper, 3)

2002, 2005–2010 (Jim Tressel, 7)

Schmidt played football at the University of Nebraska. Following law school at Nebraska and a stint in the Army, Schmidt began his head coaching career. He was head coach at Tulsa (1919–1921), Arkansas (1922–1928), and Texas Christian (1929–1933).

In 1934 Schmidt was named the head coach at Ohio State. His initial Buckeyes team went 7–1, including a 5–1 mark in the Big Ten. The following season, the Buckeyes were 5–0 in the conference and 7–1 overall. In seven years, Ohio State was 39–16–1 overall and 30–9–1 in the conference, including two titles.

RICH RODRIGUEZ

Yep, you're reading it right. A Michigan head coach among our list of favorite coaches. What's not to like about RichRod? He was 0–3 against the Buckeyes in his short-lived career, and the Wolverines were formally accused of five major rules violations while Rodriguez was in charge. Is there anyone who has left a school in shambles the way Rodriguez has?

Besides that, he wasn't that well liked. Wrote *Detroit Free Press* reporter Michael Rosenberg, "Rodriguez's staff uses some of the foulest, most degrading language imaginable. I know coaches curse, and I'm no prude, but this goes way beyond a few dirty words. He belittles his players."

In Rodriguez's debut season at Michigan in 2008, the Wolverines lost their first game to Utah and wound up 3–9, the worst record in school history. That snapped a streak of 33 consecutive bowl game appearances, the longest in the nation. Believe it or not, things got worse.

In 2009 the Wolverines were just 1–7 in the Big Ten (5–7 overall) and again sat out the bowl season. In 2010 U-M improved to 7–6, but finished seventh in the Big Ten with a 3–5 record. They lost to Mississippi State in the Gator Bowl by 38 points, the worst bowl game loss in school history.

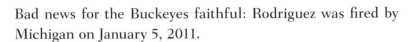

Bad news for the Buckeyes faithful: Rodriguez was fired by Michigan on January 5, 2011.

HONORABLE MENTION: LOU HOLTZ

Okay, Lou Holtz didn't play at Ohio State. (He played at Kent State.) He wasn't head coach of the Buckeyes. (He was head coach at William & Mary, North Carolina State, Arkansas, Minnesota, Notre Dame, South Carolina, and the New York Jets, compiling a record of 249–132–7.)

He was an assistant coach at Ohio State just one season. It was an important year, 1968, when the Buckeyes won the national championship. And it was a memorable year for Holtz. One of Holtz's responsibilities at Ohio State was being in charge of the practice field. Holtz said, "We were supposed to get a little bit of rain, but the field was real hard, and groundsman felt we needed a little bit of water on it, so I made the decision not to put the tarp on the field. That 'little' rain turned into a monsoon. And you get a call at 1:30 in the morning from Woody, wanting to know if the tarp was on. And you said, 'No,' and I mean…the next thing you know, he's got the whole staff our there putting the tarp on the field, ankle-deep in mud. You talk about getting a chewing out. Hey, I've been in the service, but nobody could chew you out like Coach Hayes. It's a warm memory now; it wasn't then." That was just the first of three "firings" that Holtz experienced. The other two were for missing a players' bed check and laughing during one of Hayes' tirades.

"I think Coach Hayes was the most intelligent, wide-read individual that I have ever been associated with on a continuous

UNDEFEATED SEASONS (9)

Year	Record (Conf.)	Coach
1899	9–0–1	John B. Eckstorm
1916	7–0 (4–0)	John Wilce
1917	8–0–1 (4–0)	John Wilce
1944	9–0 (6–0)	Carroll Widdoes
1954	10–0 (7–0)	Woody Hayes
1961	8–0–1 (6–0)	Woody Hayes
1968	10–0 (7–0)	Woody Hayes
1973	10–0–1 (7–0–1)	Woody Hayes
2002	14–0 (8–0)	Jim Tressel

OHIO STATE

basis," said Holtz. "I mean, the guy was absolutely a very smart individual, read incessantly—and I'm not just talking about football. I'm talking about life and politics, chemistry, history. The thing that he impressed me with was, well, several things: No. 1, a very, very fundamental individual. His football team always blocked and tackled very well. He was very simple in his approach but with very, very high standards. He would set that standard."

7

WE LOVE OHIO, COLUMBUS, AND OUR FELLOW FANS

OKAY, SERIOUSLY, what's not to like?

THE STATE

Ohio has been a major transportation hub from the Northeast to the Midwest. Bounded by Lake Erie and the Ohio River, it was a major thoroughfare for products long before the modern highway systems. Today, Ohio is within a day's drive of more than 50 percent of North America's total population.

The state is the 34th largest by area, but the seventh most populous with 11.5 million residents. The name comes from the Iroquois word *ohi-yo*, which means "great river." The state was the 17th admitted to the Union in 1803 and has traditionally been known as the Buckeye State.

After Columbus, the next largest cities in the state are Cleveland, Cincinnati, Toledo, Akron, and Dayton. Eight U.S. presidents are from Ohio, and it is one of only eight states with teams in the NFL, NBA, NHL, MLB, and MLS professional sports leagues.

The state is home to 59 of the nation's top 1,000 public companies, including Procter & Gamble, AK Steel, Abercrombie & Fitch, Goodyear Tire & Rubber, and Wendy's.

COLUMBUS

Columbus is the largest city in the state, as well as the state capital. Its population of 769,360 ranks 16th in the nation. The city is named in honor of Christopher Columbus and was founded in 1812.

Located at the confluence of the Scioto and Olentangy Rivers, Columbus is home to the world's largest clearinghouse of chemical information (Chemical Abstracts), the world's largest fractional ownership jet aircraft fleet (NetJets), the world's largest private research and development foundation (Battelle Memorial Institute), and one of the nation's largest college campuses (The Ohio State University). In addition, Columbus is home to four Fortune 500 companies: Nationwide Mutual Insurance Co., American Electric Power, Limited Brands, and Big Lots.

Besides OSU, Columbus is home to numerous other private universities and community colleges. And Columbus' professional sports teams include the Blue Jackets (NHL), Crew (MLS), and Clippers (minor league baseball).

Well-known folks from Columbus include actress Beverly D'Angelo, actor Tom Poston, boxer Buster Douglas, zookeeper Jack Hanna, Wendy's founder Dave Thomas, fighter pilot Eddie Rickenbacker, singer Michael Feinstein, dancer Twyla Tharp, guitarist Joe Walsh, and singer Nancy Wilson.

THE CAMPUS

The Ohio State University has an enrollment of 55,014 students on the Columbus campus (63,217 overall), plus 5,584 academic faculty members and 21,693 non-academic staff.

It was founded in 1870 as a land-grant university and today is the third largest university campus in the U.S. The tuition of $9,420 for the 2010–2011 academic year placed it as the fifth most expensive public school in the nation. Located on 3,469 acres, the university offers programs in 16 colleges. The central meeting point of the campus is the Oval, bordered by the Ohio

OHIO STATE

NOTED CURRENT OSU FACULTY MEMBERS

Kevin Boyle, History, 2004 National Book Award winner
Henri Cole, English, Pulitzer Prize finalist
Frank DeLucia, Physics, Max Planck Prize
Bernadine Healy, Cardiologist, former head of the National
    Institutes of Health and the American Red Cross
Eric Herbst, Physics, Max Planck Prize
Lee Martin, English, Pulitzer Prize finalist
Bebe Miller, Dance, Guggenheim Fellow
William J. Mitsch, Environmental Science, Stockholm Water Prize
Lonnie Thompson, Geology, Tyler Prize winning glaciologist
Kenneth Wilson, Physics, Nobel Laureate

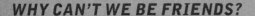

WHY CAN'T WE BE FRIENDS?

One foggy night, a Buckeyes fan is heading north from Columbus and a Michigan fan is driving south from Ann Arbor. While crossing a narrow bridge, they hit each other head-on, mangling both cars. The Michigan fan manages to climb out of his car and surveys the damage. He looks at his twisted car and says, "Man, I'm lucky to be alive!" Likewise, the Buckeyes fan gets out of his car uninjured, he too feeling fortunate to have survived. The Wolverines fan walks over to the Buckeyes fan and says, "Hey, man, I think this is a sign that we should put away our petty differences and live as friends instead of being rivals." The Buckeyes fan thinks for a moment and says, "You know, you're absolutely right! We should be friends. In fact, I'm going to see if something else survived the wreck." The Buckeyes fan then pops open his trunk and removes a full, undamaged bottle of Jack Daniel's. He says to the Wolverine, "I think this is another sign—we should toast to our newfound friendship." The Wolverines fan agrees and grabs the bottle. After sucking down half of the bottle, the Wolverines fan hands it back to the Buckeyes fan and says, "Your turn!" The Buckeyes fan calmly twists the cap back on the bottle, throws the rest of it over the bridge into the river, and says, "Nah, I think I'll just wait for the cops to show up."

Union, Wexner Center for the Arts, Enarson Hall, Kuhn Honors & Scholars House, Browning Amphitheatre, Mirror Lake, and the green space commonly called the South Oval.

WHY WE LOVE OUR FELLOW FANS

How can we close out this side of the book without a salute to the ardent supporters, newshounds, and the Internet? We can't—and we won't. There are, if you type "OSU football blogs" into your browser, 1,980,000 results. Our favorite at the

THE MOST LOYAL FAN OF ALL

Four college alumni were climbing a mountain one day: an Ohio State grad, a Michigan grad, a Penn State grad, and a Notre Dame grad. Each proclaimed to be the most loyal of all fans at his alma mater. As they climbed higher, they argued as to which one of them was the most loyal of all. They continued to argue all the way up the mountain, and finally as they reached the summit, the Notre Dame grad hurled himself off the mountain, shouting, "This is for the Fighting Irish!" as he fell to his death. Not wanting to be outdone, the Penn State grad threw himself off the mountain, proclaiming, "This is for the Nittany Lions!" Seeing this, the OSU grad walked over and shouted, "This is for the Buckeyes!" and pushed the Wolverine off the side of the mountain.

moment is buckeyecommentary.com, and "Massey" is the man of the domain. He breaks news, snaps off witty one-liners, and basically lives and breathes Ohio State football. Here's a for-instance for you:

Brady Hoke is completing his staff. The new Michigan football coach just picked up Greg Mattison as defense coordinator. Mattison previously coached in Ann Arbor from 1992–1996, the latter two years as defensive coordinator. Mattison was also the defensive coordinator for Florida in 2006. I don't need to remind you. He has spent the last two seasons as the Baltimore Ravens defensive coordinator. They are not known for their offense. So basically the guy shut down three of the best offenses OSU has ever fielded: 1995, 1996, and 2006. Hmm…I don't think I like this. You may take a slight amount of solace in the recent example set by Monte Kiffin. After all, he was a celebrated NFL defensive coordinator who returned to college football (a much longer layoff) and has yet to have the success that seemed to be preordained. And, as most average fans will tell you, Mattison is going to need at least decent defensive players first. RichRod is a lot of things; a good recruiter of defensive players is not one of them.

Still, there is reason to be concerned (or happy, depending on your perspective).... There is a sizable contingent of us that is looking forward to the Wolverines fielding a real football team on defense again soon. After all, The Game and the new Big Ten probably depends on it.

Anyone care to argue that position? You can't!

We also like blog.blockonation.com. "HD Handshoe" is its founder and owner, and he spins yarns that make you think. Who thinks of this stuff? Handshoe does, and he, too, is quite adept.

Of course, we love the numbskulls who go bare-chested in frigid temperatures, their torsos painted up in Scarlet and Gray to spell out GO BUCKS, or, the truly inventive SEND MONEY. We also love the clever imitators of Woody Hayes and Jim Tressel, who probably was singlehandedly responsible for a huge upswing in the sales of sweater vests in Ohio. Put simply, we love The Best Damn Fans in the Land. They don't jingle their keys (what the hell is *that*, Purdue?), compare literature notes (as they do in Ann Arbor), or pretend to sound like a four-legged critter (Penn State and Northwestern fans, for shame!). Buckeye Man. Frat Pack. It's a spectacle. They scream their guts out, they curse, the cheer, they can spell (listen: OH!), and they never, ever give up (IO!)

OHIO STATE

AN eBAY QUIZ

We recently typed "Ohio State Football" into eBay's search engine and, *voila*, 2,265 items came up. Items we could bid on (and some we did) included game tickets, trading cards, jerseys, autographed balls, ice scrapers, and a garden gnome. How much do you know about the value of OSU memorabilia? We tracked several listings, and here's what we discovered.

Match these items with the price that it sold for:

1. Framed color photos and autographs of all seven OSU Heisman Trophy winners
2. 1936 OSU–U-M homecoming game program
3. Eight-foot inflatable Brutus
4. 4 tickets to the 2010 OSU–U-M game (Section 26-AA, Row 6)
5. Roll of U-M football toilet paper

a. *$2,798*
b. *$700*
c. *$149.99*
d. *$99.99*
e. *$5*

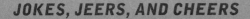

JOKES, JEERS, AND CHEERS

- How do you get a Michigan grad off of your front porch? Pay him for the pizza.
- A diehard Michigan fan and a diehard Ohio State fan are waiting to be executed. The executioner asks the Wolverine for his last request. "I'd like to hear 'The Victors' fight song one last time," he says. The executioner turns to the Buckeye and asks the same question. Without hesitation, the Buckeye says, "Shoot me first."
- What does the average University of Michigan student get on his SAT? Drool.
- At a grade school in Ann Arbor, the teacher asks the class if the Wolverines are its favorite team. All but one kid, Bobby, screams, "Yes!" The teacher asks, "Well, Bobby, who is *your* favorite team?" He says, "The Buckeyes." Astonished, the teacher asks why. Bobby says, "My parents are Buckeyes fans, so that makes me a Buckeyes fan." This agitated the teacher, who asked, "If your parents were morons, what would that make you?" Bobby replied, "A Wolverines fan."

OHIO STATE

SING ALONG WITH US, PLEASE:

We don't give a damn about the whole state of Michigan,
The whole state of Michigan,
The whole state of Michigan.

We don't give a damn about the whole state of Michigan
'Cause we're from O–HI–O.

We're from O–HI–O (OH!)
We're from O–HI–O (IO!)

We don't give a damn about the whole state of Michigan,
'Cause we're from O–HI–O (GO BUCKS!)

ABOUT THE AUTHORS

INTERESTING TO NOTE, but not germane to this manuscript (who says so? *we* do, that's who) is the fact that neither of us is a graduate of The Ohio State University. We do happen to consider it our alma mater, however.

STEVE GREENBERG is cofounder and co-owner of a chain of weekly community newspapers, Current Publishing LLC, in Carmel, Indiana. He was reared in Columbus (but he never grew up). He was a veteran editor and reporter/columnist for sports departments at daily newspapers in six states, but he didn't care much for the other 44. This is his 11ᵗʰ book. Previous titles include *I Remember Woody*, *Ohio State '68: All the Way to the Top*, and *The Game of My Life*. He is married (Sally) with college-age daughters (Annie and Rachel), loves to sail, and fronts a band, Barometer Soup, in his spare time.

DALE RATERMANN is a retired sports marketer who has written more than 40 books, including *I Remember Woody* and *Ohio State's Ohio Cross-words*. He lives in Big Ten Country and spends his retirement creating puzzles for a chain of four newspapers and watching *Ohio State's Greatest Games* on the Big Ten Network.

I
HATE
MICHIGAN

STEVE GREENBERG
& DALE RATERMANN

TRIUMPH
BOOKS

CONTENTS

1

GAMES WE HATE

No. 1: 1897

OHIO STATE	0	0	**0**
MICHIGAN	24	10	**34**

YOU KNOW WHAT THEY SAY: you never forget your first. Well, okay, nobody is still alive from a game that took place 114 years ago in Ann Arbor, so we'll just have to rely on the news accounts of the day to cry over what was the very first game in the great rivalry between Ohio State and Michigan.

By this time, U-M had been playing football for almost 20 years, while OSU was relatively new to the game, entering its eighth season of organized play. And it showed. According to the student newspaper the *Michigan Daily*:

Michigan had no trouble in defeating the Ohio State University representatives in Saturday's game. Two halves of 20 and 15 minutes respectively were played, and the score was 34–0. It was not so much Michigan's strength as Ohio's weakness that brought about the score. The visitors lined up with three of their best players absent, while Michigan put her best team on the field. While the form of the varsity team was not on the championship order, it showed an improvement over the Saturday before that was most encouraging.

Indeed, the Wolverines were coming off a scoreless tie from the previous week against that noted football power, Ohio Wesleyan. Against the Buckeyes, it was no contest. Why the game was played with one half of 20 minutes and a second of 15 is beyond us, but perhaps it was better in this case. Michigan not only dominated, but actually had a 50-yard touchdown run called back on a penalty.

It should be noted that the *Michigan Daily* made mention that, "The entire team played gentlemanly and not a single wrangle arose to mar the game."

Good to know.

No. 2: 1902

OHIO STATE	0	0	0
MICHIGAN	45	41	86

This game came in the midst of the Fielding Yost coaching dynasty in an era known as the "Point-a-Minute" teams, and it could have been worse. More on that in a moment. Obviously, this was the biggest blowout for either team in the storied rivalry. And to think, if it hadn't been for a new rule enacted by Stanford University that allowed only graduates to coach its football teams, Yost might never have made his way to Ann Arbor.

So how does it get any worse than 86–0? Well, according to OSU historian Jack Park in a story written on bucknuts.com: "You have to remember that in some of those games, touchdowns were only worth four or five points, so it's really even worse than it sounds."

Ironically, the Ohio State game wasn't even the highest-scoring game of the 1902 season for Michigan. The Wolverines edged Iowa 107–0 and slipped past Michigan State 119–0. Oh, by the way, some interesting notes about the 1902 game as reported by the *Michigan Daily*: some 6,000 people attended the contest, which seemed like a whopping crowd at the time, and 2,000 came up from Columbus by train. The paper noted that Michigan fans shouted, "What will we do? What will we do? We'll rub it in to OSU, that's what we'll do!" Clearly, the banter back and forth between the fans has been enhanced since then.

Also, a fascinating little tidbit that most certainly sums up the values and modesty of the time as compared to today: during the game, an Ohio State player had his jersey completely torn off. Players from both teams formed a human screen around the player while he changed into a new jersey so nobody from the crowd could see him.

Finally, there was something of a silver lining that came out of the 86–0 loss for OSU—freshman player Fred Cornell wrote "Carmen Ohio" on the train ride home to Columbus.

Michigan's Tom Harmon (98) breaks loose for a long gain against Ohio State at Ann Arbor on November 25, 1939. Harmon's all-around play helped the Wolverines defeat the Buckeyes 21–14 that day and then 40–0 the next year.

No. 3: 1940

MICHIGAN	13	7	13	7	40
OHIO STATE	0	0	0	0	0

In the long and famous history of Michigan–Ohio State, there have been many incredible individual achievements. One of the first, and maybe still the greatest, was that of Michigan's Tom Harmon. Harmon was Everybody's All-American long before *Sports Illustrated* writer Frank Deford wrote his book of the same name, which was loosely based on former Louisiana State star Billy Cannon.

Harmon, the father of actor and *NCIS* star Mark Harmon, was Michigan's first Heisman Trophy winner. In 1940 he rushed for 852 yards, passed for 506, and had 21 total touchdowns. His season was punctuated on November 23, 1940, against the Buckeyes at Ohio Stadium, when he scored two rushing touchdowns, threw for two TDs, rushed for 139 yards, passed for 151 yards, kicked four extra points, and intercepted three passes, including one he returned for a touchdown. "Old 98" broke the all-time college scoring record held by the legendary Red Grange of Illinois.

"I saw Tom Harmon play, and he was no doubt a pure Heisman Trophy winner," former Michigan tackle Alvin Wistert said in the 2003 Pat Summerall–produced and –narrated documentary, *Rivalries: The History of Michigan–Ohio State.* "He did everything. He punted, he passed, he received kickoffs, he received punts, he played both offense and defense…. He was a great football player and a great person."

Added Michigan All-America halfback Bob Chappuis in the same film: "Tom Harmon was my idol. He was a senior at Michigan when I was a senior in high school. He was probably the best all-around football player that I ever saw. He did the whole thing. And he was fast."

For his efforts in that 1940 game against the Buckeyes, Harmon not only clinched the Heisman Trophy but received something that, to this day, is extraordinary—a standing ovation from the Ohio State faithful at Ohio Stadium. Perhaps it was for the amazing game, or amazing career. In three games against Ohio State, Harmon accounted for 618 yards—238 more than OSU as a team.

No. 4: 1950

MICHIGAN	2	7	0	0	9
OHIO STATE	3	0	0	0	3

One of the most remembered games of the series, recalled less for the outcome or for memorable plays—there weren't any—but instead for the simple fact that the game took place in one of the worst blizzards in Ohio history.

It has come to be known as the Snow Bowl.

The weather was truly awful—*dangerous* might actually be the better term—and since it was OSU's home game, the school had the option of postponing the contest, or even canceling the game and retaining the Big Ten championship. OSU was ranked eighth in the country at the time; Michigan was unranked. Still, the winner was heading to the Rose Bowl.

To their credit, the Buckeyes decided to play—although Fritz Crisler's very clear admonition certainly had something to do with it. Crisler, then Michigan's athletics director, told his counterpart at OSU, "If we don't play today, I'm not coming back next week."

It was certainly nothing to write home about. The game, that is. The weather certainly was. The contest was played in near white-out conditions with temperatures at 10 degrees at kick-off with a 29-mph wind, making it feel like −12.

The referees desperately tried to sweep and shovel snow off the yard lines, but the blizzard was relentless. It resulted in a whopping 45 punts between the two teams. Michigan didn't complete a pass, didn't gain a first down, and gained 27 yards on the day. Ohio State had three first downs and gained 41 yards.

Special teams proved to be the difference. Ohio State's Vic Janowicz, that year's eventual Heisman Trophy winner, kicked a 27-yard field goal to give the Buckeyes a 3–0 lead. But the Wolverines came back and blocked one of his punts, which squibbed out of the end zone for a safety, trimming the deficit to 3–2.

Late in the second quarter, Ohio State coach Wes Fesler decided to punt on third down. It wasn't unusual—the weather was so bad and field position was so key that both teams had actually punted on first down on occasion during the game. In fact, Michigan quick-kicked on the first play of the game.

But this particular decision by Fesler to punt proved disastrous.

"I'm sitting up there because I'm kind of a redshirt guy and not dressed for the game," recalled former Ohio State player and Coach Earle Bruce, "and I'm sitting behind a little old lady about 83 years old, and she jumps up and says, 'Don't you punt that ball, Fesler! Don't you dare punt that ball!' I jumped up and said, 'I'm with you, lady. Don't punt the ball!' We punted the ball. They blocked it. We lost the game 9–3, and Fesler never coached another game."

Of course, the game simply could not be remembered without having a classic Michigan–Ohio State twist attached to it. Brothers Robert and Tony Momsen were squaring off against each other in the game, and as fate and irony would have it, both played pivotal roles.

Robert "Buckeye Bob" Momsen recovered a blocked Michigan punt early in the game that set up Janowicz's field goal that gave OSU a 3–0 lead. But it was Michigan's Tony Momsen who scored the game's decisive, and only, touchdown, when he chased down the punt that the Wolverines blocked on OSU and fell on it in the end zone for the score.

No. 5: 1969

OHIO STATE	6	6	0	0	**12**
MICHIGAN	7	17	0	0	**24**

This one is arguably the worst game in the history of the rivalry. The backstory—there's always a backstory with Michigan–Ohio State, right?—was what led to this not only being considered the worst game of the rivalry, but also one of the greatest games in college football history and, ultimately, a game that ABC television announcer Bill Flemming ended by saying, "There it is! What has to be the upset of the century!"

Ohio State came into the game as the defending national champions under Woody Hayes and with a 22-game winning streak. The Buckeyes were considered unbeatable. More important, just the year before, OSU had beaten Michigan 50–14—and, late in the game, Hayes made the decision to go for a two-point conversion with his team up by five touchdowns. When asked by reporters afterward why he went for two, Hayes replied, "Because I couldn't go for three."

It was also the first season of coaching at U-M for a former Hayes assistant who went on to make his mark as a head coach at Miami of Ohio, drawing the attention of the University of Michigan—Glenn E. "Bo" Schembechler.

And the new guy never let the Wolverines forget what had happened the year before.

"When we went to our locker room to get our equipment, we saw the number 50 everywhere," former Michigan offensive lineman Dick Caldarazzo said. "Bo had put 50 on everything you could see. All the shower curtains were 50, there was a 50 on everybody's locker."

"That stuck in the craw of the Michigan players," Schembechler said. "You know, when you have an intense rivalry that's very close and one game gets out of hand and you rub it in like that, it'll come back to haunt you."

Legend has it that Schembechler told his players, "Get me through the first 30 minutes with a lead, and I'll beat the old man in the next 30 minutes." And that's how it played out. All 36 points were scored in the first half. Ohio State drew first blood when it pinned Michigan deep in its own half of the field, got the ball back in good field position, and scored on a one-yard run by Jim Otis to take a 6–0 lead after a missed extra point.

The teams traded scores on the next two possessions. Michigan went up 7–6, but the Buckeyes came right back and drove down the field to take a 12–7 lead. (The Bucks kicked the

PAT, but when Michigan was called offside, Hayes went for two and failed.)

Then the key sequence: the Wolverines started the next possession at their own 33-yard line and methodically drove to OSU's 33. Schembechler called for a tailback draw, and Billy Taylor gained 28 yards on the play to set up a touchdown that put U-M ahead for good, 14–12.

Michigan held the Buckeyes to a three-and-out on the next possession, forcing a punt that Barry Pierson returned 60 yards to OSU's 3-yard line, setting up another score that made it 21–12. After stopping Ohio State yet again, Michigan drove from its own 36 to OSU's 3-yard line again, settling for a field goal and the final points of the half—and the game.

Legendary U-M radio broadcaster Bob Ufer said at the end of the broadcast, "Ripley couldn't have written it any better than this!"

"We played a tremendous game at Iowa the week before, and not many people realize that Iowa is not that bad a team," Schembechler said after the game. "In the locker room, we talked about beating Ohio State even before we took our uniforms off….We took the field against Ohio State, and that was the most enthusiastic football team I've ever been associated with."

At a 40-year reunion of the game in 2009, Schembechler's widow, Cathy, said, "Of all the boys Bo coached, the '69 team was the one he was closest to and remained close to forever. He meant a lot to them, and they meant a lot to him."

No. 6: 1986

MICHIGAN	3	3	13	7	26
OHIO STATE	14	0	3	7	24

Call it the Jim Harbaugh Game. Everybody remembers this one for what was, at the time, still considered a bit of a brash statement, especially in the college ranks—a guarantee by Harbaugh, Michigan's starting quarterback, that the Wolverines would beat the Buckeyes at Columbus in their annual encounter.

Harbaugh made the statement in the aftermath of a shocking loss to Minnesota the week before, the team's first of the year, and he backed it up by going 19-for-29 for 261 yards against the Buckeyes.

But in reality, it was the Jamie Morris game. Morris rushed for a career-high 210 yards, 150 in the second half, and scored two touchdowns. "You know, you have to go back to the week before," Morris recalled. "We went to Minnesota, and we got caught looking ahead to Ohio State. We watched film of Minnesota, but, you know, as young kids sometimes do, we saw it and thought that Minnesota wasn't that good, and it would be easy. And we got beat."

It was something that head coach Bo Schembechler actually feared, Morris said. "He saw how we had practiced before the Minnesota game, and he said it in his pregame speech, 'I hope this week doesn't hurt us,'" Morris recalled. "The funny thing that not many people know about that game is, this was going to be Bo's [166th] victory at Michigan, the most of any Michigan coach. So we got a plaque already, before the game, and we were going to present it to Bo. But we lost, so we had to scrape off the 'Minnesota' and put 'Ohio State' in there."

So when Michigan went into Columbus a week later, "We were all very quiet, very somber, very serious about the game," Morris said. "We had just lost our undefeated season and our No. 2 [national] ranking. We knew we were a better team than what we showed against Minnesota."

Morris said Schembechler came into his hotel room the night before the game and said, "I need you to visualize. I need you to see yourself doing good things with the ball." Morris paused, laughed, and said, "And, of course, we got down 14–3 right away."

TOP 5 U-M PASSING GAMES VS. OSU

1. **Tom Brady** | 375 yards | 1998
   31-for-56, TD | 31–16 (OSU)

2. **Chad Henne** | 328 yards | 2004
   27-for-54, 2 TDs | 37–21 (OSU)

3. **Drew Henson** | 303 yards | 2000
   14-for-25, 3 TDs | 38–26 (U-M)

4. **John Navarre** | 278 yards | 2003
   21-for-32, 2 TDs | 35–21 (U-M)

5. **Chad Henne** | 267 yards | 2006
   21-for-35, 2 TDs | 42–39 (OSU)

MICHIGAN

Michigan was still down 17–13 when Morris took over. His 52-yard run set up his own eight-yard TD run to put U-M up 19–17 after a missed two-point conversion, and Morris had the bulk of the carries on an 85-yard drive that resulted in Thomas Wilcher's seven-yard score for a 26–17 advantage.

As for Harbaugh's bold prediction of victory, Morris said the team backed their senior quarterback 100 percent. "As a player, you like to see your leader making a statement like that," Morris said. "He believed in that team. That's his senior year. He made a statement that we were going to win. Bo was pissed, because it was bulletin board material that would fire Ohio State up. In the pregame meeting, Bo said, 'Our quarterback shot his mouth off, so we have to go out there and back it up.' He didn't like it, but we needed that kick in the pants. We needed Jim to say that."

No. 7: 2003

OHIO STATE	0	7	7	7	21
MICHIGAN	7	14	7	7	35

This game at Ann Arbor, as big a game as they come, was the 100th game in the history of the storied rivalry. It's also the last game in the series that Michigan has won to date. The 100th game in the history of the series naturally was accompanied by huge pomp and circumstance and media coverage. ABC announcer Keith Jackson did the voiceover for the intro to the game, and it was, of course, magnificent:

This is a remarkable festival annually whether here or at the Horseshoe. There are the great bands. "Fight that team across the field, show 'em Ohio's here..." "Hail to the victors valiant, hail to the conquering heroes..." Today, another bounty of memories concluding a hundred years of Buckeyes and Wolverines.

Both quarterback John Navarre and tailback Chris Perry had big games for Michigan. The former threw for 278 yards and two touchdowns; the latter rushed for 154 yards and scored twice against an Ohio State defense that was giving up an average of just 50.4 yards rushing per game. And once again, it was another season in which the loss denied Ohio State a likely chance to play in the national championship game. Navarre rallied his team to a 35–21 victory, and Michigan was off to its first outright Big Ten championship and Rose Bowl in six years.

No. 8: 1997

OHIO STATE	0	0	7	7	**14**
MICHIGAN	0	13	7	0	**20**

This is one of the ones that we continue to lose sleep over. This is the year where the tables were turned. It was Michigan this time that came into the game undefeated and ranked No. 1, and it was No. 4 OSU looking to spoil the season and prevent the Wolverines from going to the Rose Bowl and playing for the national championship.

The Wolverines took a 20–0 lead in Ann Arbor and held on for the six-point victory in a game that not only capped an undefeated season, but clinched the Heisman Trophy for Charles Woodson. Just three weeks after Woodson had had another big game on national TV in the 34–8 win over Penn State that

catapulted U-M into the No. 1 spot in the polls, Woodson—
primarily a defensive player—caught a 37-yard pass that set up
one score and ran back a 78-yard punt for a touchdown. He
also intercepted a pass while performing his day job as one of
the top lockdown cornerbacks in the country.

This was also the game that wide receiver David Boston failed
to learn from history. Boston was quoted during the week
leading up to the game, saying that he played against defensive backs every day in practice who were better than Woodson, and predicted a Buckeyes victory. Boston did catch a long
touchdown pass from Stanley Jackson, but for the most part
was not a factor—and, in what became an iconic cover photo
on *Sports Illustrated*, Boston was shown being laid out in mid-
air by a great hit from Michigan safety Marcus Ray.

"Charles Woodson is the greatest player I've ever been around,"
former Michigan coach Lloyd Carr said. "He made every single guy that was around him better. If his best friend wasn't
working hard, Charles Woodson would not spare him."

No. 9: 1995

OHIO STATE	3	6	6	8	**23**
MICHIGAN	7	3	7	14	**31**

No. 9a: 1996

MICHIGAN	0	0	10	3	**13**
OHIO STATE	3	6	0	0	**9**

We put these games together because, well, you can't hate one
without hating the other. And it marked the beginning of the

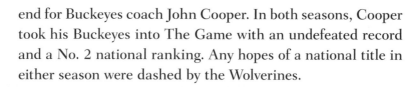

end for Buckeyes coach John Cooper. In both seasons, Cooper took his Buckeyes into The Game with an undefeated record and a No. 2 national ranking. Any hopes of a national title in either season were dashed by the Wolverines.

The 1995 game at Ann Arbor was basically a one-man show, while the 1996 game at Columbus was a collective effort on the part of the defense. In 1995 it was all Tshimanga "Tim" Biakabutuka, who rushed for a whopping 313 yards—still a record for most individual rushing yards in a Michigan–Ohio State game—and the Wolverines beat the Buckeyes 31–23.

"I'm obviously disappointed," OSU coach John Cooper said after the game. "I don't know if I've ever been as disappointed in my life as I am right now." Somebody should have warned him about the '96 game.

Biakabutuka broke off a 22-yard run on the game's first play and never looked back. Ohio State wide receiver Terry Glenn had guaranteed a victory earlier that week by saying the Buckeyes would be playing in the Rose Bowl.

Glenn dropped two balls in the game, and instead, it was Northwestern that ended up in its first Rose Bowl game in 46 years. And, in a bit of Shakespearean foreshadowing, a true freshman by the name of Charles Woodson intercepted two passes in the game.

A year later, in 1996, the Buckeyes came in with another juggernaut team and expectations of playing for the national championship. And for the better part of two-plus months, that's how it played out. OSU was unstoppable, or so it seemed. The

TOP 5 U-M RUSHING GAMES VS. OSU

1. **Tim Biakabutuka** | 313 yards | 1995
   37 carries, TD | 31–23 (U-M)

2. **Jamle Morris** | 210 yards | 1986
   29 carries, 2 TDs | 26–24 (U-M)

3. **Rob Lytle** | 165 yards | 1976
   29 carries, TD | 22–0 (U-M)

4. **Jim Pace** | 164 yards | 1957
   22 carries | 31–14 (OSU)

5. **Tom Kuzma** | 162 yards | 1941
   30 carries | 20–20 (tie)

MICHIGAN

Buckeyes scored less than 27 points just once all season entering the Michigan game—a 17–14 win over Wisconsin—and twice rolled up 70 points. They were as good on the road as they were at home, scoring wins at No. 5 Notre Dame—yes, back when Notre Dame was good—at Purdue, and at No. 20 Iowa.

This time, two forces combined—Mother Nature and defense. The U-M defense held the Buckeyes to just nine points. And Mother Nature provided a bit of a slippery field, or at least in one spot where OSU All-America safety Shawn Springs fell down on a simple 10-yard pass from Brian Griese to Tai Streets, who bolted the last 59 yards to paydirt on the second play of the second half that catapulted Michigan to the victory. At the time, the Wolverines trailed 9–0. That cut it to 9–7, and U-M added two second-half field goals while the defense held OSU to 84 yards in the second half. Once again the loss ended an unbeaten season for the Buckeyes and any shot at a national championship. At the time, neither the Big Ten nor the Pac-10 was part of the fledgling Bowl Alliance, and both its champions were obligated to play in the Rose Bowl, to which OSU was still headed.

"It's sickening, it's an awful feeling," Ohio State fullback Matt Calhoun said after the game. "I thought I can't have this type of feeling again, and here I am feeling it again."

"We have had a good year, but it's not a great year when you don't beat Michigan," Cooper said.

Michigan safety Marcus Ray summed it up best when he said, "I'd rather not go to the Rose Bowl and beat Ohio State, than go to the Rose Bowl and not beat Ohio State."

2

PLAYERS WE HATE

DESMOND HOWARD

DESMOND HOWARD WAS an all-state running back at St. Joseph High School in Cleveland. He opted to go to Michigan and played wide receiver for the Wolverines from 1989 to 1991. In his three seasons up north, the Wolverines were 3–0 against the Buckeyes.

In those three games versus Ohio State, Howard had eight receptions for 169 yards and one touchdown, one rush for eight yards, two kickoff returns for 51 yards, and two punt returns for 107 yards and one TD, which we'll get to shortly.

Howard was the first receiver in Big Ten history to lead the league in scoring. He set or tied five NCAA records and 12 single-season U-M records. Howard was named the MVP of Super Bowl XXXI and is the only special-teams player to win

Michigan wide receiver Desmond Howard (21) strikes the "Heisman" pose moments after scoring on a 93-yard punt return in a 31–3 trouncing of Ohio State in 1991 at the Big House. Photo courtesy of Getty Images

the award. He is one of four players to win the Heisman Trophy and Super Bowl MVP.

Granted, he was a talented football player. But it's not his statistics and laurels that got him onto our list of players we hate. It was The Pose. In The Game in 1991 (a contest the Wolverines won 31–3) Howard scored on a 93-yard punt return. He didn't act as if he'd done it before (he had) and just hand the ball to the official. He didn't spike the ball. He struck The Pose. Not just any pose, but the Heisman Trophy pose as depicted by Ed Smith on the actual trophy. Smith, a New York University football player of note, modeled for the trophy's sculptor with a ball tucked under one arm, the other arm extended with his legs spread wide. The Pose. Howard did win the Heisman Trophy that year. In a landslide.

When he isn't still striking The Pose today, Howard can be seen as an ESPN college football analyst. (But not by us.)

CHARLES WOODSON

Another all-state running back from Ohio who headed up north was Charles Woodson. Ohio's Mr. Football at Ross High School, Woodson played for the Wolverines from 1995 to 1997. He was primarily a defensive back in college, but returned kicks and lined up as a wide receiver in certain situations.

HEISMAN TROPHY WINNERS/ SUPER BOWL MVPs (A SHORT LIST)

		Heisman Trophy	Super Bowl MVP
1.	Roger Staubach	1963 (Navy)	VI (1972— Dallas Cowboys)
2.	Jim Plunkett	1970 (Stanford)	XV (1981— Oakland Raiders)
3.	Marcus Allen	1981 (USC)	XVIII (1984— Los Angeles Raiders)
4.	Desmond Howard	1991 (Michigan)	XXXI (1997— Green Bay Packers)

MICHIGAN

As a freshman, the Michigan DB had two interceptions against the No. 2–ranked Buckeyes in Michigan's 31–23 win. As a sophomore, the Wolverines won 13–9. And as a junior, Woodson returned a punt for a touchdown, had an interception in the end zone, and a 37-yard reception that led to the Wolverines' only offensive TD of the game. Michigan won 20–14, en route to the national championship.

Woodson won the Heisman Trophy following his junior season in 1997, making him the first primarily defensive player to win. He bypassed his senior season (yay!) and was selected fourth overall in the NFL Draft. He has played for Oakland (1998–2005) and Green Bay (2006–present) and has been a seven-time Pro Bowl selection. Woodson was the NFL Defensive Player of the Year in 2009.

TOM BRADY

Tom Brady was a quarterback on a college team that won a national championship. He guided an NFL team to an undefeated regular season and has won three Super Bowls. Women think he's gorgeous. And he's married to a supermodel. Okay, admit it. You really wish you could be Tom Brady.

So, what's to hate? He's a Michigan Man.

Brady didn't play against Ohio State in 1995 (a redshirt season), 1996, or 1997 (all Michigan wins), but he did play against the Buckeyes as a junior and senior. In 1998 the Buckeyes beat Brady and the Wolverines 31–16. But he completed 31 of 56 passes for 375 yards and one touchdown. The completions, attempts, and yards were all U-M single-game passing records.

TOM BRADY'S PASSING STATS
AS A WOLVERINE

Over his two seasons as a starter for Michigan, Tom Brady compiled some impressive passing statistics, though nothing that would have foreshadowed the record-setting, Super Bowl–winning future he'd have in the NFL. His career college stats:

443-for-711 (62.3 pct.) | **5,351 yards**
35 TDs | **19 INTs**
136.4 NCAA passer rating (90.6 NFL rating)
20–5 record as starter, including **2–0** in bowl games

MICHIGAN

In 1999 Brady completed 17 of 27 passes for 150 yards. In typical Brady fashion, he threw two TD passes in the final 15:07 to lead Michigan from a 17–10 deficit to a 24–17 win.

Said another Michigan star, Ty Law, "Tom was somewhat slighted, but it gets to the point that you get used to it. It's been that way for him. But what do stats mean if you're sitting at home for the Super Bowl? Winning is the trump card for everything. Tom Brady is the greatest winner in football right now."

Said Brady, "You always want to be perfect out there. But it's really about improving all parts of the game and trying to be more efficient." If that's what it takes to land a supermodel and star in the NFL, sign us up.

DENARD ROBINSON

Let's go straight to the head-to-head numbers:

2009: Ohio State 21, Michigan 10; 2-for-4 passing for three yards and no TDs; 10 carries for 31 yards and no TDs.

2010: Ohio State 37, Michigan 7; 8-for-18 passing for 87 yards and no TDs; 18 carries for 105 yards and no TDs.

That's no touchdowns and two Michigan losses in two games versus Ohio State. Nada. Zip, zilch, zero. A big goose egg. Is this the same guy who pulled a Desmond Howard and struck the Heisman Trophy pose after scoring a touchdown against Notre Dame? Is this the guy who was selected as the Big Ten's Offensive Player of the Year in 2010?

JUST CALL HIM "SHOELACE"

To everyone in his hometown of Deerfield Beach, Florida, Denard Robinson is known as "Shoelace." He got the name for his habit of not tying his shoes, even on the football field.

Said his high school coach, Art Taylor, "After 25 years coaching, if the kid can throw it 90 yards in the air and is accurate, and the kid can run as fast as he does...as long as he feels comfortable not lacing his shoes, fine with me. The kid's been doing it all his life, why mess with it?"

MICHIGAN

Okay, his numbers and records in 2010 were downright gaudy against the rest of the world: NCAA record for most rushing yards by a quarterback in a season (1,702). First player in NCAA history to throw for 2,000-plus yards (2,570) and run for 1,500-plus yards (1,702) in a season. Against Notre Dame alone, he set Michigan records for total yards (502) and most rushing yards in a road game (258), set a Big Ten record for most rushing yards in a game by a QB, and became only the ninth player in NCAA history to both rush and pass for more than 200 yards in a game.

He did just finish his sophomore season. And now maybe he has a real coach to draw up and call plays that will utilize his skill set. But it's tough to like a guy who hasn't shown much to the Ohio State faithful and gets the rest of the nation in a tizzy.

At Deerfield Beach (Florida) High School, Robinson recorded a 40-yard-dash time of 4.32 and ran a leg on the Florida high school state championship 4 x 100 relay team. But he was rated just the 35th best overall college football prospect in the state of Florida by Rivals.com, one of the leading scouting services.

Robinson played in all 12 games for Michigan as a freshman, including one as the starting running back. He played well, but did not rack up any numbers that would give an indication of what the future held. But in the 2010 season opener, Robinson set school records for total offense (383) and rushing yards by a quarterback (197). And the stats and honors kept piling up.

TSHIMANGA BIAKABUTUKA

This one's personal. You try typing *Tshimanga Biakabutuka*—as opposed to, say, Ty Law—every few pages. Two of Dale's fingers are sporting Band-Aids, our computer's spell-check now goes out twice a week to see a psychiatrist, and our editor has deleted ~~Tshimanga Biakabutuka~~ his name from the book ~~four~~ five times.

But we keep bringing him back, not because of his name, but because of what he did to the Buckeyes. We know you'd rather forget, but let us remind you why he's on our hate list. It was 1995, and Ohio State was undefeated heading into the final regular season game at Ann Arbor. Biakabutuka almost single-handedly beat the Buckeyes, rushing for 313 yards and one touchdown on 37 carries. The Wolverines won 31–23. That remains the most rushing yards by any back in any game in the OSU–U-M series. It's the second-highest rushing total for a game in Michigan's history (behind Ron Johnson's 347 yards in a 1968 game against Wisconsin). The 313 yards wasn't a fluke. Biakabutuka ran for 1,818 yards that season, the best single season in Wolverines history.

He was typically modest following the game. "I've been playing football for six years, and even in high school I never saw holes that big. Anybody could have run through those holes and gained all those yards," he said.

Buckeyes coach John Cooper was disheartened. "We didn't wrap up," he said. "Time and time again we had guys there to make the tackle, but we didn't wrap up. I'm tremendously disappointed. I don't know if I've ever been as disappointed as I am right now."

Biakabutuka left his native Zaire with his family at the age of four. They settled in Canada, near Montreal, which enabled the youngster to play football in school and earn a scholarship to Michigan. "Touchdown Tim" was a first-round draft pick of the Carolina Panthers. He rushed for 2,530 yards and caught 77 passes for 789 yards in his six-year NFL career.

TOM HARMON

This has to be a misprint. Archive records indicate that "in an unprecedented display of sportsmanship and appreciation, the Ohio State fans in Columbus gave Harmon a standing ovation at game's end." The guy just led the Wolverines to a 40–0 pasting of the Buckeyes in the Horseshoe. He scored three touchdowns on the ground, threw for two more, kicked four extra points, intercepted three passes, and averaged 50 yards on three punts. And our fans cheered him?

Many give Tom Harmon the title of Greatest Michigan Football Player Ever. That alone deserves jeering from the Scarlet and Gray. Harmon was a three-sport sensation in high school in Indiana and played football and basketball at U-M from 1938 to 1940. He was a tailback in a single-wing offense and the team's kicker and punter. In three seasons, he rushed for 2,134 yards, threw for 1,304 yards and 16 touchdowns, and scored 237 points. He also played in the defensive secondary. Twice he led the nation in scoring.

He was awarded the Heisman Trophy in 1940, and since then, his life has been far removed from Indiana and Ann Arbor. He was the first player chosen in the NFL Draft, but played with the New York Americans in the upstart American Football

THE HARMON FAMILY BIZ

In 1944 Tom Harmon married actress Elyse Knox, who'd starred in *The Mummy's Tomb* opposite Lon Chaney Jr., among other films. (Her wedding dress was made from the silk parachute Harmon used to bail out of a crippled plane over occupied China during the war.) They had two daughters, Kristin, an actress who married recording artist Ricky Nelson; and Kelly, an actress who married car czar John DeLorean. (Kristin's daughter, Tracy Nelson, is also an actress, and her twin sons, Gunnar and Matthew, are musicians.) Tom and Elyse also had a son, Mark, who was a starting quarterback at UCLA and is still working as an actor. Mark was named the "sexiest man alive" by *People* magazine in 1986, has been the star of *NCIS* since 2003, and is married to actress Pam Dawber.

League instead. He took a turn in Hollywood, playing himself in the aptly named biopic *Harmon of Michigan*. He enlisted in the Army Air Corps and was awarded the Purple Heart and Silver Star for his actions in World War II. He returned to civilian life and played two seasons for the Los Angeles Rams in the NFL. He dabbled as an actor and was one of the first athletes to make the transition from the field to the press box, working in sports radio and television broadcasting.

Tom Harmon was later known as "Old 98" for the number he wore at Michigan. He suffered a heart attack after winning a golf tourney at the Bel-Air Country Club and died in 1990 at the age of 70.

THE WISTERTS
WHITEY, OX, & MOOSE (AKA LARRY, MOE, & CURLY)

Even though very few of you were around when the brothers Wistert were pounding our Ohio State lads, their story is too good for us to ignore. It's a story that begins in Chicago. The family was of Lithuanian descent, and their father was killed in the line of duty while working for the Chicago Police Department. But the three sons persevered.

First, there was Francis "Whitey" Wistert. He was a star high school athlete who went to Michigan. He wore No. 11 and was an All-America tackle on the football team that won three consecutive Big Ten championships (1931–1933). He also was the Big Ten's MVP in baseball in 1934 and played briefly in the big leagues.

Second, there was Albert "Ox" Wistert. He was a star high school athlete who went to Michigan. He wore No. 11 and was an All-America tackle on the football team from 1940 to 1942. He played nine seasons in the NFL, earning All-Pro honors eight times. His teams won two NFL titles.

Third, there was Alvin "Moose" Wistert. He was a star high school athlete who went to Michigan at the age of 31 after trying his hand at several occupations. He wore No. 11 and was an All-America tackle on the football team that won three consecutive Big Ten championships (1947–1949). He remains the oldest All-American ever selected (33 years old).

Michigan retired uniform No. 11 in honor of all three Wisterts. All three are in the College Football Hall of Fame. They combined for a 5–2–2 record against the Buckeyes.

Later, Alvin quipped, "If I'm not mistaken, I think this is unprecedented in the annals of college football—that three brothers all would go to the same school, all played football, all played tackle, all wore the same No. 11, all made All-American. Two of us played on four national championship teams. And all were inducted into the College Football Hall of Fame."

BENNIE OOSTERBAAN

Bennie Oosterbaan was a three-time All-America football end, a two-time All-America basketball player, and an All–Big Ten baseball player at Michigan from 1925 to 1928. He was the Big Ten touchdown leader in football, the Big Ten scoring champion in basketball, and the Big Ten batting champion in baseball. So when did he find time to study? He must have. He also was awarded the Western Conference (Big Ten) Medal of Honor for proficiency as a scholar-athlete.

As a player, Oosterbaan's U-M football teams were 3–0 against the Buckeyes. In the dedication game of Michigan Stadium in 1927, Oosterbaan threw three touchdown passes to lead the Wolverines to a 21–0 win over Ohio State. When Oosterbaan graduated, he passed on a pro football career. He grew up in the Dutch Reformed Church. Said Oosterbaan, "Dutch Reformed didn't play football on Sundays." Instead, he got into coaching. He was an assistant football coach at U-M for 20 years before replacing Fritz Crisler as the head coach in 1948. He remained in that position for 11 seasons. He was the school's head basketball coach from 1938 to 1946. And he was the coach of the freshman baseball team for several years.

Oosterbaan's football team won the national championship his first season, and U-M won Big Ten titles in each of his first three seasons. Overall, he was 63–33–4. He was 5–5–1 against OSU. In basketball, he was 81–72 overall (3–9 versus Ohio State). After stepping down as football coach, he held a number of positions in the U-M athletics department until he retired in 1972. He died at an Ann Arbor nursing home in 1990 at the age of 84. In 1969 Oosterbaan was chosen as one of the 11 greatest players in the first 100 years of college football. In 2003 *Sports Illustrated* named him the fourth greatest athlete in the history of the state of Michigan (behind Joe Louis, Magic Johnson, and Charlie Gehringer). His jersey No. 47 was the first one retired at U-M. And in 1954 he was inducted into the College Football Hall of Fame.

Oosterbaan may have been the ultimate Michigan man. As one obituary noted, he "went to Ann Arbor as a freshman in 1924—and never left."

RON KRAMER

Ron Kramer won nine varsity letters at Michigan from 1954 to 1957. He was a two-time All-American in football, set the school career scoring record in basketball, and was a high jumper for the track team.

On the gridiron, Kramer was versatile. At various times in his collegiate career, he played defensive end, receiver, running back, quarterback, punter, and place-kicker. His uniform

No. 87 was retired following his senior season. On the basketball court, he was the team MVP three consecutive seasons, captain of the squad as a senior, and scored a school record 1,119 points in his career (since broken). For all his individual success, Kramer's U-M teams didn't fare well against the Buckeyes. Michigan was 1–2 in football and 2–2 in basketball in the Kramer era.

In the NFL, Kramer was a prototypical tight end. He played several years for Green Bay under Vince Lombardi and three seasons for Detroit. He was named All-Pro twice and played on two NFL championship teams. Said Kramer's football coach, another three-sport U-M star, Bennie Oosterbaan, "To top off his marvelous physical gifts of size and speed and strength, plus an uncanny coordination, Kramer was one of the fiercest competitors I've ever seen. Nothing was impossible for him— the impossible was only a challenge."

DAN DIERDORF

Dan Dierdorf didn't need directions to the Pro Football Hall of Fame in Canton, Ohio, when he was enshrined in 1996. He was born in Canton and played football at Glenwood High School (now GlenOak High School).

However, Dierdorf went to Michigan, instead of Ohio State. He starred as an offensive tackle at Michigan from 1968 to 1970. The Wolverines were 25–6 overall during his career, but were just 1–2 against the Buckeyes. Michigan won the Big Ten title in 1969, and he was a consensus All-American in 1970. Dierdorf was chosen by the St. Louis Cardinals in the second round of the NFL Draft. The Cardinals' offensive line had the reputation of being the dirtiest in the league. He played 13 seasons for the Cardinals, earning Pro Bowl honors six times. He was selected by his peers as the top NFC offensive lineman three years running (1976–1978).

Following his playing career, the always opinionated Dierdorf got into broadcasting. In 1987 he joined the *Monday Night Football* announcing team and remained there for 12 seasons. After he was let go by ABC, he was hired by CBS and has been doing NFL games since.

ANTHONY CARTER

No. 1 on your scorecard and No. 1 in the hearts of many Michigan fans, Anthony Carter was a touchdown machine for the Wolverines from 1979 to 1982. He had a school record 40

10 *MONDAY NIGHT FOOTBALL* ANNOUNCERS WE'D RATHER LISTEN TO THAN DAN DIERDORF

1.	Frank Gifford	6.	Fran Tarkenton
2.	Don Meredith	7.	Alex Karras
3.	Al Michaels	8.	Dan Fouts
4.	John Madden	9.	Lynn Swann
5.	Howard Cosell	10t.	O.J. Simpson
			Dennis Miller

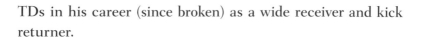

TOP 5 U-M RECEIVING GAMES vs. OSU

1. **Braylon Edwards** | 172 yards | 2004
   11 catches, TD | 37–21 (OSU)

2. **Marquise Walker** | 160 yards | 2001
   15 catches, 2 TDs | 26–20 (OSU)

3. **Braylon Edwards** | 130 yards | 2003
   7 catches, 2 TDs | 35–21 (U-M)

4. **Anthony Carter** | 125 yards | 1979
   2 catches, TD | 18–15 (OSU)

5. **Tai Streets** | 118 yards | 1998
   9 catches, TD | 31–16 (OSU)

TDs in his career (since broken) as a wide receiver and kick returner.

So what made Carter such a favorite of the Wolverines faithful? Maybe it was his size. He was listed at 5′11″, 160 pounds. Maybe it was that his presence made the run-happy Wolverines throw the ball—at least some. Besides his scoring records, he also finished his career as No. 1 on U-M's career lists in receptions, receiving yards, punt returns, punt return yards, kickoff returns, and kickoff return yards. He was a two-time team MVP, a three-time All-American, and the Big Ten's MVP as a senior. He finished in the top 10 in the Heisman Trophy voting three consecutive seasons, finishing fourth as a senior.

Ohio State fans are still trying to figure out the hype. Carter scored just two of his 40 career TDs against the Buckeyes. And he had zero points against Ohio State in his junior and senior seasons. In fact, in his career, he had just as many tackles against the Buckeyes (on interception returns) as he had TDs.

In his four seasons against OSU, he had zero rushing yards on one carry, 17 catches for 302 yards and two TDs, seven kickoff returns for 218 yards, and eight punt returns for 77 yards. The Wolverines were 1–3 against the Buckeyes and didn't score more than 15 points in any game.

Prior to the NFL Draft, Carter signed with the upstart USFL. As a result, he slid to the 12th round and was the 334th player selected. He played three seasons in the USFL with the Michigan Panthers/Oakland Invaders before joining the NFL in 1985. He showed flashes of his college days in catching 486 passes and scoring 55 touchdowns over 11 NFL seasons (nine with Minnesota and two with Detroit), but failed to reach the end zone as a kickoff and punt returner in the regular season.

JIM HARBAUGH

Jim Harbaugh guaranteed that Michigan would beat Ohio State in 1986. For that alone he has the undying hatred of Buckeyes fans (although his comments about his alma mater's academics and his decision to spurn U-M in 2011 and take the head coaching position with the San Francisco 49ers has elevated his stock a bit among OSU faithful).

Harbaugh has to be on this list. He was a three-year starter for Bo Schembechler, though he broke his arm and missed

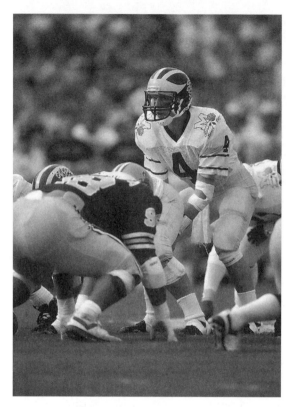

After guaranteeing a win against Ohio State and backing it up on the field in 1986, Michigan quarterback Jim Harbaugh led his Wolverines to the Rose Bowl, where they lost to the Arizona State Sun Devils 22–15. Photo courtesy of Getty Images

the last six games of his sophomore year in 1984, including a 21–6 loss to Ohio State. Harbaugh came back and beat OSU in 1985 and then, in 1986, after the unbeaten Wolverines were stunningly upset at Minnesota, Harbaugh said this: "I guarantee we will beat Ohio State and go to Pasadena."

In 2007 Harbaugh told *USA Today*, "The way our leader, Bo Schembechler, handled it was genius. He just came into the team meeting, and I'm kind of expecting to get an earful. He said, 'Well, at least I know our quarterback thinks we can win. Rally around him. Let's go to Columbus and beat the Buckeyes.'" Michigan won 26–24.

Harbaugh led the nation in passing efficiency in 1985, guiding the Wolverines to a 10–1–1 mark; in 1986 he was the Big Ten Player of the Year and third in the Heisman Trophy balloting after an 11–2 campaign.

RICK LEACH

Like Ron Kramer, Rick Leach was a gifted and extraordinary athlete. Leach was an All-American in football and baseball. He was a four-year starter from 1975 to 1978 for Bo Schembechler, a left-handed dream who could not only throw the ball but could run it. He set a then–NCAA record for most touchdowns accounted for (82) and broke Big Ten records for total offense (6,460 yards), total plays (1,034), and touchdown passes (48).

At the beginning of his sophomore year in 1976, Leach ended up on the cover of *Sports Illustrated*'s college football preview issue. And there was no jinx—sophomore, cover boy, or any other. Beginning that season, Leach led Michigan to three consecutive wins over Ohio State and three straight trips to the Rose Bowl.

When it was all said and done, Leach was drafted as a senior by not one, not two, but three teams—the NFL's Denver Broncos, the Montreal Alouettes of the Canadian Football League, and baseball's Detroit Tigers. He opted to pursue a career in baseball, playing 10 years for four different teams.

JAMIE MORRIS

Jamie Morris was just 5'7". Initially, Coach Bo Schembechler didn't recognize that. When Morris arrived on campus for his freshman year in 1984, Bo recalled for the *New York Times* that, "I told Jamie when we recruited him he was too small to be a running back and we wanted him for running back kicks. I did, however, promise him the chance to try to be a running back for us. Good thing I did, isn't it?"

Morris was inserted into the starting lineup as a tailback three games into his freshman season and never came out. In his four-year career, he became the first player to ever lead the Wolverines in rushing four straight seasons, a mark since tied by Mike Hart. He rushed for 1,703 yards in his senior season, the third best total in U-M history.

A versatile player, Morris also caught 99 career passes for 756 yards and is fifth on the all-time school list for kickoff return yardage. He finished with 6,201 all-purpose yards.

But Morris' best game came against—you guessed it—Ohio State during his junior year. Morris ran for 210 yards, had 22 yards receiving, and 70 yards in kick returns for 302 all-purpose yards in Michigan's 26–24 victory.

JON JANSEN

One of the great offensive linemen in Michigan history, Jansen started 50 consecutive games at right tackle for the Wolverines, a school record. It's quite an achievement if you think about it. Like players before him who were known for their longevity (Rick Leach, Anthony Carter, Tom Harmon, etc.), Jansen needed a combination of factors to do it, includ-ing remaining injury free, being good enough to start as a freshman, and having the luxury of playing 12- and 13-game seasons that included an NCAA-allowed extra game and, of course, a bowl game.

A two-time team co-captain, Jansen was the Big Ten Offensive Lineman of the year in 1998 and was also named GTE/CoSIDA Second-Team Academic All-America. He received Michigan's Big Ten Medal of Honor for his academic and athletic achievements. Jansen is best known for being the rock that held Michigan's line together in the 1997 national championship season. The Wolverines were 3–1 against Ohio State in his four seasons.

BOB CHAPPUIS

Bob Chappuis began his University of Michigan career in 1942, played one season for the Wolverines, and then was drafted into the U.S. Army for World War II. He flew 21 missions as a radio operator and aerial gunner during his three-year stint in the service, and his plane was shot down in northern Italy on his 21st mission. Chappuis and two other crew members survived and were hidden by Italian resistance members for three months, until the war in Europe ended in May 1945.

Chappuis then returned to play football at Michigan and, despite missing three years, simply excelled. Chappuis led Coach Fritz Crisler's 1947 "Mad Magicians" to a 10–0 record, including a win over Ohio State—another W over the Buckeyes would come in the 1948 season—and a 49–0 win over USC in the Rose Bowl. Chappuis earned All-America honors as well as Rose Bowl MVP honors as the Wolverines captured the Associated Press national championship in a bit of a controversial selection over Notre Dame.

Chappuis was featured on the cover of *Time* magazine that year as well in an article titled "The Specialist," which talked about Crisler's decision to specialize the offensive and defensive units at U-M. At a time when virtually every player went both ways, playing offense and defense, Crisler separated the two squads into 11 different players on each side of the ball.

Chappuis briefly played professional football in the All-America Football Conference in 1948 and 1949, but instead of jumping to the NFL, he retired when the AAFC folded. He is a member of the College Football Hall of Fame.

HARRY KIPKE

He played at U-M. He coached at U-M. He was a regent for the university. Anything that had even a remote hint of maize and blue, and Harry Kipke was there.

Like Ron Kramer, Kipke was a nine-time letter-winner at Michigan—three in football, three in basketball, and three in baseball. He was an All-American in football in 1922 and widely considered to be the best punter of his time and one of the best in school history. During his three-year career, Kipke helped Michigan to a 19–1–2 record, a 2–1 record against Ohio State from 1921 to 1923, and the 1923 national championship.

As a coach, Kipke led the Wolverines for nine seasons and went 46–26–4, including back-to-back national championships in 1932 and 1933. Along with Fielding Yost—for whom he played—and Bo Schembechler, Kipke is one of just three men to have coached Michigan teams to four consecutive conference championships.

ROB LYTLE

Sadly, Rob Lytle passed away on November 21, 2010, at the age of 56. He is remembered as the great player he was—an All-America running back at Michigan who had a stellar career for the Maize and Blue and went on to score a touchdown in the Super Bowl in 1978 as a rookie with the Denver Broncos. "He was one of the toughest guys I ever played with and one of the best leaders, who made the ultimate sacrifice for us by playing fullback at times," former teammate Rick Leach told the Associated Press after Lytle's death.

Lytle was the Big Ten's MVP and an All-American in 1976 when he finished third in the Heisman Trophy balloting

U-M's NATIONAL CHAMPIONSHIPS (11)

Don't get too excited, Wolverines fans, four of these came before the invention of the forward pass. Only one has come since the Korean War.

	Record	(Conf.)
1901	11–0	(4–0)
1902	11–0	(5–0)
1903	11–0–1	(3–0–1)
1904	10–0	(2–0)
1918	5–0	(2–0)
1923	8–0	(4–0)
1932	8–0	(6–0)
1933	7–0–1	(5–0–1)
1947	10–0	(6–0)
1948	9–0	(6–0)
1997	12–0	(8–0)

MICHIGAN

behind Pitt's Tony Dorsett and Southern Cal's Ricky Bell. Lytle rushed for a total of 3,317 yards and 26 touchdowns from 1973 to 1976. The 1976 team beat Ohio State and went to the Rose Bowl.

"Rob was a teammate and an incredibly terrific guy," Michigan athletics director David Brandon said in a statement. "It's a sad day because we've lost someone who was a great example of a Michigan man."

JON RUNYAN

Jon Runyan was an All–Big Ten offensive lineman for Michigan in 1995, wrapping up a career that included 34 starts and two victories in three years over Ohio State. He was a 1996 fourth-round draft pick of the Houston Oilers and went on to play 14 years in the NFL before turning his attention to politics.

In 2010 he ran for New Jersey's Third Congressional District seat and ousted Rep. John Adler in the race, assuming his place in the House of Representatives. Runyan has been a board member for the Alzheimer's Association of South Jersey and five times has hosted the "Score for the Cure" golf tournament, which benefits prostate cancer research.

BRIAN GRIESE

At the end of the 1998 Rose Bowl, after Michigan beat Washington State to clinch a perfect 12–0 season, there was the looming question of whether it would be the Wolverines or the Nebraska Cornhuskers who deserved to be national champions. Michigan quarterback Brian Griese, who was asked

GRIESE vs. GRIESE

Comparing Father and Son Grieses' Pro Careers:

Bob (Purdue)

1967–1980 (Miami) | Pro Football Hall of Fame (1990)
Pro Bowl (1967, 1968, 1970, 1971, 1973, 1974, 1977, 1978) |
    All-Pro (1971, 1977)
1,926-for-3,429 (56.2 pct.) | 25,092 yards | 192 TDs, 172 INTs
77.1 (passer rating) | 92–56–3 (record)

Brian (Michigan)

1998–2002 (Denver), 2003 (Miami), 2004–2005, 2008 (Tampa Bay),
    2006–2007 (Chicago)
Pro Bowl (2000)
1,752-for-2,796 (62.7 pct.) | 19,440 yards | 119 TDs, 99 INTs
82.7 (passer rating) | 45–38 (record)

about that very scenario after the game, said, "I don't know what more we can do. I ask you, what more can we do?"

Griese will forever be remembered as the quarterback who delivered the school's first national title in 50 years when the Wolverines were named Associated Press national champions for their unbeaten 12–0 1997 season.

Griese, a walk-on who eventually earned a scholarship, had a brilliant campaign, completed 62.9 percent of his 307 passes that year for 2,293 yards, 17 touchdowns, and just six interceptions. He capped it with a 251-yard, three-touchdown performance against the Cougars in the Rose Bowl.

TYRONE WHEATLEY

Tyrone Wheatley was a three-time All–Big Ten selection and ranks fourth on the Michigan career rushing list with 4,178 yards. He also scored 47 touchdowns, good for second on the all-time list. Wheatley still holds the Michigan single-season yards-per-carry record (7.34 in 1992). His U-M teams were 2–1–1 versus Ohio State from 1991 to 1994, though his 1994 senior season was marred by a shoulder injury that made him less than 100 percent.

Wheatley was drafted by the New York Giants and played 10 years in the NFL. He completed his first year as the running backs coach for Syracuse University in 2010.

THE GLORIOUS BASTARDS
WHICH SIDE DID YOU SAY YOU WERE ON?

It's tough to say anything bad about someone who served in the military. (At least someone who fought on your side.) Someone who puts his life on the line to defend your freedom is top-notch in our book. But in this case, we'll make an exception. Okay, two exceptions.

Consider the cases of Howard Yerges Jr. and John "J.T." White. Howard Jr. was the son of Howard Yerges, who played for Ohio State in the 1910s and then professionally for the Columbus Panhandles in 1920. Junior was a standout quarterback for Grandview High School in Point Pleasant, West Virginia, and enrolled at OSU, where he lettered in 1943. The following year, as a U.S. Navy trainee, Yerges was forced to transfer to the University of Michigan. He joined the Wolverines football team and served as the backup QB, earning a letter. Yerges remained the backup but took over the starting role late in the 1945 season when the No. 1 QB was injured. He was the starter when U-M beat Ohio State 7–3.

In 1946 Yerges started five games, but shared time with Pete Elliott and Jack Wiesenburger. Yerges and U-M petitioned the conference office (then the Big Nine) for a fifth season of eligibility and received it, excusing his playing time at Ohio State. (Excuse me?)

Yerges started nine of the 10 games in 1947, leading the Wolverines to an undefeated season (including a 21–0 beatdown of the Buckeyes), a Rose Bowl win, and the national championship. In the Rose Bowl, a 49–0 Michigan win over Southern Cal, Yerges threw a touchdown and caught a TD pass. Following his graduation, Yerges took a job in the automobile industry, then worked as a sales executive in St. Louis.

White, on the other hand, grew up in River Rouge, Michigan, but chose Ohio State to play both football and basketball. He lettered in both sports for the Buckeyes, playing center for the 1942 football team that ended the season ranked No. 1 in the nation and forward and center for the basketball team. In 1943 White enlisted in the U.S. Army and served three years. Upon his discharge, White enrolled at Michigan, where his younger brother, Paul, was captain of the football team. White started at center for two years, earning second-team All-America honors from the Football Writers of America. He anchored the offensive line that helped the Wolverines go 10–0 and win the national championship in 1947. Thus White played on national championship football teams at both Ohio State and Michigan.

He passed on an opportunity to play pro football and got into coaching instead. He was an assistant at Michigan from 1948 to 1953 and at Penn State from 1954 to 1979.

Yerges and White remain the only two players—at least since World War II—who started their careers at Ohio State and ended them at Michigan.

TRAITORS TO OHIO

Players from Ohio on the 2010 Michigan Roster:

	Yr.	Pos.	Hometown (H.S.)
Courtney Avery	Fr.	CB	Mansfield (Lexington)
Isaiah Bell	Fr.	LB	Youngstown (Liberty)
Jibreel Black	Fr.	DE	Wyoming (Wyoming)
Curt Graman	Fr.	C	Cincinnati (Elder)
Kevin Koger	Jr.	TE	Toledo (Whitmer)
Jordan Kovacs	So.	S	Curtice (Clay)
Elliott Mealer	So.	OL	Wauseon (Wauseon)
Brandon Moore	So.	TE	Trotwood (Trotwood-Madison)
Patrick Omameh	Fr.	OL	Columbus (St. Francis DeSales)
Christian Pace	Fr.	OL	Avon Lake (Avon Lake)
Jerald Robinson	Fr.	WR	Canton (South)
Roy Roundtree	So.	WR	Trotwood (Trotwood-Madison)
Jake Ryan	Fr.	LB	Westlake (St. Ignatius)
Michael Shaw	Jr.	RB	Trotwood (Trotwood-Madison)
Terrence Talbott	Fr.	CB	Huber Heights (Wayne)
Terry Talbott	Fr.	DT	Huber Heights (Wayne)
Fitzgerald Toussaint	Fr.	RB	Youngstown (Liberty)
Ray Vinopal	Fr.	S	Youngstown (Cardinal Mooney)
D.J. Williamson	Fr.	WR	Warren (Warren G. Harding)

MICHIGAN

3
TRADITIONS WE HATE

GO BLUE BANNER

CLEMSON HAS ITS ROCK, Florida State has its burning spear, Oklahoma has its Sooner Schooner. Michigan has its banner. A banner? Yeah, a banner. And they brag about that? Although the tradition is relatively new—introduced in 1962—the 30-foot long, five-foot high blue banner with the maize lettering that spells out GO BLUE with "M Club Supports You" underneath is one of the most recognizable traditions and game-day entrances in college football.

The Wolverines gather in the tunnel on the east side of Michigan Stadium, bunching together like a herd of wild horses waiting to be sprung free, and then make a mad dash for midfield, where they run under the banner, reaching up to touch it as they head toward the home sideline.

The 2011 season marks the 50th year of the tradition, and there are a couple of different, yet intertwined, origins of how

47

Michigan players jump up to slap the "Go Blue" banner before getting slapped down even harder by the Buckeyes 21–10 on November 21, 2009, in Ann Arbor.

it all came about. According to the school's official website, mgoblue.com, "Though the Graduate 'M' Club made the permanent banner, it was the Undergraduate Club that started the tradition with a simple yellow block 'M' on a six-foot wide strip of fabric. On the Friday practice before the 1962 team's homecoming game against Illinois, the 'M' Club assembled all the non-football letter-winners to form two lines as the players ran off the field toward the locker rooms in Yost Field House. The club was given permission by then coach Bump Elliott to form the flag tunnel before the game the next day, and the rest is history."

But when the Michigan fan blog Those Who Stay Will Be Champions recounted the origins of the banner back in 2007 on its site, Judy Renfrew Hart, daughter of former Michigan hockey coach Al Renfrew, responded with a comment of clarification: "Just so you know, the tradition was started by Al Renfrew and Marguerite Renfrew. Marge was asked by Al to make two flags to drape over the Yost football locker rooms to cheer on the team. She made two flags with a neighbor, Mrs. Helmers. The Block M was designed by Bob Hoisington, an engineering dean, to make sure it was correct. They handmade the flags, which was not an easy feat at the time. They had the M Club members hang them over the Yost locker room to begin with, later it was moved to the tunnel at the stadium. After the games they came back home…and were hung at their house. Later it was changed to a banner. Al still [has] one of the original flags, with the football on the top of the flagpole."

So, like the banner, the stories of its origins are a bit frayed.

The Go Blue banner quickly became ingrained as a Michigan fixture, both in the hearts of U-M fans and in the minds of the opposition. Twice the banner has been stolen and in 1973 came the infamous incident when Ohio State came out of the tunnel at Michigan Stadium and tore down the banner. As Joel Pennington recalled in his book *The Ten Year War: Ten Classic Games Between Bo and Woody*, normally the Buckeyes would come out of their tunnel and turn left to gather in front of their own sideline. But OSU player John Hicks went straight toward midfield, and the Buckeyes pulled down the banner being held by Michigan students and began jumping up and down on it. They quickly dispersed, but the incident left legendary Michigan radio voice Bob Ufer in a tizzy.

"Here they come: Hare, Middleton, and the Buckeyes…and they're tearing down Michigan's coveted M Club banner! They will meet a dastardly fate here for that! There isn't a Michigan man who wouldn't like to go out and scalp those Buckeyes right now. They had the audacity, the unmitigated gall, to tear down the coveted M that Michigan's going to run out from under!… But the M-men will prevail because they're getting the banner back up again. And here they [the Michigan team] come! The Maize and Blue! Take it away, 105,000 fans!"

Instead of running straight out through midfield under the banner, when Michigan took the field, the Wolverines broke right and amassed in a group huddle in front of OSU's sideline before heading to their own sideline, back underneath the banner that had been quickly raised again.

Alas, the histrionics and emotions on both sides went for naught—the 1973 game ended in a 10–10 tie.

THOSE WHO STAY WILL BE CHAMPIONS

It's more than just a sign on a wall or a coach's mantra. It's a creed. It's a belief. It's dogma. It's a way of life.

When Bo Schembechler was hired to coach the University of Michigan football team, the memory of a 50–14 humiliation by Ohio State in the 1968 game was fresh in everyone's mind. But so too was the fact that the Wolverines had won just one Big Ten championship between 1951 and 1968, that coming in 1964. That was an 18-year stretch that was hard to digest for U-M fans, especially with Ohio State and Woody Hayes competing for—and winning—Big Ten titles and national championships. So, when legendary athletics director Don Canham went looking for a new coach to replace Bump Elliott, he

THE VICTORS WALK

At press time, it was unknown whether new Michigan coach Brady Hoke would incorporate much from the Rich Rodriguez regime, but one of the traditions the new coach will probably keep is the Victors Walk.

This wasn't Rodriguez's baby; a version of the Victors Walk had been instituted by Coach Bump Elliott in the 1960s and kept up by Bo Schembechler for a few years after he took over in 1969, but RichRod brought it back in 2008.

While not as elaborate as the Grove at Ole Miss, the Victors Walk is a 200-yard walk by the Michigan football players from the east side of Crisler Arena, through the parking lot and the cheering fans and tailgaters, to the locker room entrance at Michigan Stadium.

MICHIGAN

focused squarely on Schembechler, who was enjoying success at Miami of Ohio.

When Schembechler took over, he had a sign placed in the training room: Those Who Stay Will Be Champions. Little did any of the players know what was in store for them. If the ESPN-produced movie *The Junction Boys* captured the difficulties of the Texas A&M training camp in the searing Texas heat under Coach Bear Bryant, well, the winter and spring of 1969 in Ann Arbor, weren't far behind.

In George Cantor's book, *I Remember Bo...*, offensive lineman Dick Caldarazzo said of Schembechler, "He beat the crap out of us those first few months of 1969. The walk-ons were dropping like flies. We had to run a mile in under six minutes, jump the stadium stairs on one leg, then jump upstairs on one leg with a teammate on your back. We hated it and we hated him."

Dave Rentschler, who played at Michigan in the mid-1950s, became friendly with Schembechler from his days as a former M Club president. He told Cantor for the book that there was a method behind Schembechler's madness.

"These were someone else's players," Rentschler said. "Bo didn't recruit them. He had to find out in a hurry whom he could count on and whom he could trust. He set out to make sure the others left. That's why he put up the famous sign: 'Those Who Stay Will Be Champions.' Everyone who ever played for Bo always remembers that sign."

The Wolverines started with about 140 players at the beginning of winter workouts and spring ball. By the time the team reconvened that summer to begin training camp in preparation for the season, the roster was down to roughly 80 players. Or, to be exact, 80 survivors.

Cantor himself wrote that Schembechler was an anathema to the times, and therefore to the players. Remember, this was 1969—Vietnam, the counterculture movement—and Ann Arbor and the University of Michigan campus were at the center of the Midwest's portion of the firestorm.

Not for Schembechler, though.

"In an era when we were all being told to do our own thing, whatever that was supposed to mean, and when anyone who advocated a disciplined life was regarded as a fascist, here was this guy who refused to bend," Cantor wrote, "who was uncompromising in his belief that doing things the tough way was the only right way."

Thomas Takach, a 1969 letter-winner who stayed, said that players were leaving the program left and right. "One afternoon between classes during spring practice, I decided to come in early in order to have my ankles taped for practice later that same day," Takach recalled for a 2009 article on the school's website commemorating the 40-year anniversary of the 1969 Big Ten champs. "As I arrived in the old football training room–locker room complex—which were adjacent areas on the second floor of Yost Fieldhouse—I found that the locker room was dark and completely deserted except for one person, John Prusiecki, a big defensive lineman from Indiana. He had just quit, and after informing the coaches of his decision had come in to clean out his locker. Failing to realize that he was not alone, he had taken a Sharpie pen and, below the words 'Those Who Stay Will Be Champions' on Bo's sign, had added 'and those who leave will be doctors, lawyers, and scientists.' Eventually, most of the team saw the graffiti before the sign was replaced.

"That sign stating, 'Those Who Stay Will Be Champions' remained in the locker room throughout spring practice, individual summer workouts, and the entire fall football season," Takach continued. "It became a primary, philosophical, motivating force for that team during the 1969 championship season and for future teams, as well, summarizing the driving force and encompassing the goals of the entire group of athletes who wear the maize and blue. As usual, it turned out that Bo was right—those who stayed did become champions. We were the 1969 Big Ten football champions and the Big Ten representative in the Rose Bowl on January 1, 1970."

Caldarazzo said the team finally realized what the mantra meant in the 1969 win over Ohio State. "We controlled the game in the second half," he said. "I thought back to all those stupid conditioning drills and realized this is what it was all for. They couldn't keep up with us."

At the memorial at Michigan Stadium following Schembechler's death in 2006, Dan Dierdorf recalled the famous saying and found its deeper meaning. "Those of us in 1969, we were the first people that ever heard that phrase here in Ann Arbor," the former U-M lineman said. "When Bo said, 'Those who stay will be champions,' that phrase really means that if you stayed with Bo, you would be a champion—not just when you were wearing the helmet of the Michigan Wolverines, but you would be a champion for the rest of your life."

MICHIGAN

IN MICHIGAN, IT'S PRONOUNCED "LI-BARY"

If you visit the website for the Bentley Historical Library (www.bentley. umich.edu) for Michigan literary space junk, you'll be as tickled by this as we were. When you click on the link for "Michigan vs. Ohio State," you immediately are transported to civilization...and the site for The Ohio State University Library (http://library.osu.edu/projects/ OSUvsMichigan). Bahahahahaha! Skippy and Buffy can't even do their own work—they have to mooch off Ohio State.

GOLF COURSE TAILGATING

Across the street from Michigan Stadium is the Michigan golf course, which in all seriousness, could double as a goat ranch. But on select Saturdays during the fall, it hosts several hundred cars and thousands of Michigan football fans on its fairways.

While there are spots within spitting distance of the stadium that have great tailgating, including the Crisler Arena parking lot, which sits just behind the east side of the stadium, the golf course is the place to be.

For a noon game, the gates open at 8:00 AM. Hint: enter from State Street, cross the 1st fairway and park on the 9th fairway. It's a great time and a great atmosphere, especially if you're into a more sophisticated tailgate (read "hoity-toity") as opposed to the drunken frat brothers routine elsewhere on campus.

The only downside? You have to exit the golf course two hours after the conclusion of the game, which doesn't leave a heck of a lot of time for the U-M faithful to drown their sorrows after a loss. But, then again, if you play your cards right for a 3:30 PM start, you'd be able to eat three meals on the course!

And the Michigan Golf Course isn't the only place to park. Adjacent to the college course is the nine-hole Ann Arbor Golf & Outing Club, which is also an excellent place to tailgate or graze your extra goats. It holds more than 1,500 cars at $40 a pop. Or, if you know somebody who knows somebody who knows somebody, you can always park in somebody's driveway or on their lawn. Remember, Michigan Stadium looks like it was picked up and dropped into the middle of a residential neighborhood in Ann Arbor. While some homeowners clearly enjoy their privacy, others are practitioners of the great American pastime of capitalism. Some charge $50, $60, even upwards of $100 to park on their lawn and/or driveway, and some have longstanding, yearly customers who are more than willing to pay the steep price for the privilege of literally walking across the street to Michigan Stadium.

One homeowner, who shall remain nameless, gets $50 a car and is able to park eight cars a game on his property. "You do the math," he said. "That's $400 a game times six to eight games a year. That pays for my vacation." (To where? Not a bowl game, that's for sure.)

THE WINGED HELMET

Okay, we'll give them this: the University of Michigan's football helmet has to be one of the most instantly identifiable symbols in intercollegiate athletics. It also makes us kind of vomit in our mouths.

The famous "winged" design—which really doesn't have anything to do with Wolverines, unless they fly...but we can't confirm that—dates to 1938 when Coach Herbert O. "Fritz" Crisler arrived from Princeton. Even as the design and composition of helmets evolved from stitched cowhide to high-tech, molded plastic, the winged design has remained the preeminent symbol of Michigan football. The hideous headgear debuted against Michigan State in 1938, a 14–0 U-M victory. The *Michigan Alumnus* reported, "Michigan has a fighting gridiron outfit once more; a team that knows how to do things and a burning desire—and considerable ability—to do what it

The Michigan winged helmet, the symbol of Michigan football, was actually pilfered from Princeton in 1938. Also, the wings have nothing to do with wolverines, which are foul-smelling, filthy weasels.

wants." Oddly, none of the newspaper accounts of the game make mention of the new helmet. Probably too embarrassing. (Fighting gridiron outfit? Puh-leeze.)

The winged helmet is *the* symbol of Michigan football, even greater perhaps than the block M. Back in the day, virtually every school wore the same kind of headgear, usually a black or brown leather helmet. As the game progressed and the helmets became more advanced for safety, they nonetheless bore a resemblance to each other.

But when Fritz Crisler arrived at Michigan from Princeton in 1938, his sense of style and design came with him. "Michigan had a plain black helmet and we wanted to dress it up a little," Crisler recalled in a long-ago interview recorded by the U-M Bentley Historical Library. "We added some color [maize and blue] and used the same basic helmet I had designed at Princeton."

Ah, but it was more than that. Crisler also believed that the helmet design would make it easier for Michigan quarterbacks to spot Wolverines receivers down the field. "There was a tendency to use different-colored helmets just for receivers in those days, but I always thought that would be as helpful for the defense as for the offense," Crisler recalled. And he was right. According to the school's website, from the 1937 to 1938 seasons, Michigan nearly doubled its passing yards, cut its interceptions almost in half, improved its completion percentage, and went from 4–4 in 1937 to 6–1–1 in 1938.

Now, the winged helmet is not only used by the Michigan football team, but by the U-M hockey team, catchers for the baseball and softball teams, field hockey goalies, even the swim team's racing caps.

NO. 1 JERSEY

Arguably, the No. 1 jersey is the most coveted uniform number in Michigan football. (Is it because most of the players have a hard time remembering any number larger?)

While six players wore No. 1 from 1919 to 1978, the jersey was made most famous and most popular by three-time All-America wide receiver Anthony Carter, who wore it during his career from 1979 to 1982.

Since then, it has been reserved for a wide receiver and has become something of a privilege to be given the No. 1 jersey—and with it, an acknowledgment of a certain level of talent and an expectation that the recipient will live up to its lofty status.

The No. 1 jersey is so important in Michigan lore that it actually ignited a public firestorm when Rich Rodriguez was the U-M coach. During the off-season of 2008, Rodriguez gave the No. 1 jersey to incoming freshman defensive back J.T. Floyd of Greenville, South Carolina. This upset former Wolverines wide receiver Braylon Edwards, who wore No. 1 at U-M and who had endowed a generous $500,000 scholarship to the athletics department for the Michigan player worthy of wearing the No. 1 jersey. Edwards was so upset that he went public in May 2008, telling ESPN's Mike Tirico (an Ann Arbor resident) on Tirico's radio show: "I'm glad you gave me a Go Blue question because RichRod gave the No. 1 jersey to an incoming freshman DB, and the No. 1 jersey has never been

PLAYERS WHO HAVE WORN NO. 1 AT MICHIGAN

	Pos.	Years Worn
Angus G. Goetz	LT	1919–20
Robert Jerome Dunne	G	1921
Paul G. Goebel	E	1922
Harry Kipke	HB	1923
Dave Whiteford	DB	1973–1975
Gregg Willner	K/P	1976–1978
Anthony Carter	WR	1979–1982
Greg McMurtry	WR	1986–1989
Derrick Alexander	WR	1990–1993
Tyrone Butterfield	WR	1994–1996
David Terrell	WR	1998–2000
Braylon Edwards	WR	2003–2004

MICHIGAN

worn by anybody outside of a wide receiver. It dates back to Anthony Carter, [Greg] McMurtry, Tyrone Butterfield, Derrick Alexander, David Terrell, and yours truly. So I'm going to have a talk with him about that the next time I see him. He's getting that call soon—very soon.... We have a jersey scholarship fund for this whole deal. What is he thinking?"

The disagreement was eventually sorted out, although Rodriguez probably didn't do himself any favors when he admitted he did not know the history and tradition of the No. 1 jersey, nor did he know of Edwards' scholarship endowment. The former coach switched Floyd's jersey to No. 12, but Edwards still harbored resentment. In a January 2010 game between his New York Jets and the Cincinnati Bengals on NBC's *Sunday Night Football*, Edwards introduced himself as "Braylon Edwards, [from] Lloyd Carr's University of Michigan."

MICHIGAN STADIUM

Michigan Stadium is located at the corner of Main Street and Stadium Boulevard in Ann Arbor, Michigan. From six to eight fall Saturdays a year, Michigan Stadium becomes the state of Michigan's fourth-largest city for a few hours when more than 109,000 people pack the place to watch the Wolverines play football. And, as in the state's three largest cities, the unemployment rate for the crowds exceeds 20 percent.

The stadium is a bowl, and three-quarters of it is underground. That was part of the vision of Fielding Yost when he conceived of the stadium, allowing for easier expansion. Michigan Stadium, though technically part of the university's athletics campus, looks like it was plunked down in the middle of a

The "Big House"—Michigan Stadium—in Ann Arbor, with another 100,000-plus sellout crowd of Wolverine-lovin' fans. Just a big bowl of wrong.

residential neighborhood. In fact, it was, though the reality is that the 'hood sort of built up around the stadium, which was built in 1927. Today, traveling north on Main Street leads you into the heart of downtown; south takes you to I-94, the major interstate that leads to both Detroit and to Chicago and points west. But traveling east on Stadium Boulevard takes you past the University of Michigan golf course, Crisler Arena, and into a cluster of houses and apartments; going west on Stadium takes you through a leafy neighborhood with abandoned couches on the curb and abandoned cars on concrete blocks.

According to U-M Bentley Library Archives, in 1893 "the Athletic Field," later known as Regents Field, opened with a capacity of 400. In 1902 Detroit businessman Dexter Ferry donated 21 acres of land to the university just north of the Athletic Field, and the Regents changed the name of the complex to Ferry Field. Four years later, a new field was built on that land and served the Michigan football team for two decades.

And then Fritz Crisler came along and convinced everyone—especially potential bondholders who were asked to pay $500 each, a staggering sum in 1926, for the construction of a new stadium—of the great potential of this sport of football. Crisler worked his magic, and Michigan Stadium was built in time for the 1927 season, with 70 rows of seating and a capacity of 82,000, which included the addition of some wooden bleachers.

On October 1, 1927, the Wolverines won their first game at the new facility by defeating Ohio Wesleyan 33–0. Three weeks later, in the dedication game, Michigan beat Ohio State before a then–Michigan Stadium record crowd of 84,401.

From there, here are some notable events in a timeline of the Big House:

1928
Stadium capacity is upped to 85,753.

1930
Michigan becomes the first stadium to erect electronic scoreboards at both ends of the stadium.

1946
Michigan breaks the half-million mark in a season for the first time with 514,598 fans.

1949
Capacity is raised to 97,239 and, in

the first year that NCAA attendance records are kept, Michigan leads the nation with an average of 93,894 for each of its six home games.

1956

Capacity increased again, to 101,001. On October 6 of that year, Michigan Stadium hosts more than 100,000 people for the first time, as 101,001 see the Michigan State game.

1969

On October 4, the Wolverines lose at home to Missouri, 40–17. Michigan would not lose another game at home until November 22, 1975, a streak of 41 games.

1973

Capacity is increased again, this time to 101,701.

1975

On November 8, Michigan shuts out Purdue 28–0. The more noteworthy item, however, is that 102,415 fans show up, starting a streak of 100,000-plus attendance that continues to this day.

1996

The Champions Plaza was added, and brick pillars and wrought-iron fencing were installed around the stadium perimeter.

1998

An expansion adds another 5,000 seats to increase official capacity of 107,501. But the new seating area is surrounded by a yellow parapet bearing familiar Michigan icons, including the winged helmet, the university seal, and words from "The Victors." It is universally despised, and fans come to call the monstrosity "the Halo."

1999

The Wolverines play their 150th consecutive game in front of at least 100,000 fans with a 37–3 win over Rice on September 11.

2000

"The Halo" is removed as then–school president Lee Bollinger acknowledges that "the depth of the criticism and concern seemed to be genuine and coming from reasonable people."

2003

In the season finale, a 35–21 win over Ohio State in the 100th meeting between the two teams, Michigan sets the NCAA single-game attendance mark as 112,118 spectators file through the gates.

2004

In the longest game in Big Ten history, Michigan rallies from 17 down in the fourth quarter to beat Michigan State in triple overtime, 45–37.

2006

U-M plays its 200th consecutive game with at least 100,000 fans in attendance, a win over Ball State, coached by none other than Brady Hoke. That gives the new U-M coach a 0–1 lifetime record in Michigan Stadium as a head coach, a mark even RichRod is envious of.

2007

The final portion of the bleachers restoration is completed, and the school announces a new, three-year renovation project of Michigan Stadium that will add premium, luxury seating and a new press box.

2010

The three-year construction project is completed in time for a September 4 rededication of Michigan Stadium.

MICHIGAN

01

Michigan Stadium has undergone several renovations in the last decade or so, including the installation of the infamous and much-derided "Halo" that ringed the stadium in the late 1990s (and lasted only two seasons); the installation of video scoreboards, also in the late 1990s; and a renovation of the stadium to install a new press box on the west side and premium seating on the east side of the facility that was completed in time for the 2010 season.

But every time they fix up the old girl and have to remove or add some seating, there is one constant: capacity at Michigan Stadium will always end in "01."

That's a nod to former athletics director and football coach Fritz Crisler, who was AD in 1956 when Michigan Stadium was expanded to its 101,001 capacity. The plus-one has traditionally been the extra, honorary seat for Crisler.

HAIL TO THE VICTORS

"The Victors" is a catchy little ditty that neither strikes fear into the heart of Buckeye Nation nor…well, never mind, as this is a semi-family book. Louis Elbel and the Regents of the University of Michigan own the copyright for the lyrics. There's a part where they sing "the leaders and the best." Of what? At what? Anyway, that drivel doesn't apply anymore, not since the Big Ten instituted the insidiously idiotic divisional names, Leaders and Legends. Michigan had best get the chaps down in rewrite to make over these lyrics; the Wolverines, you see, are members of the Legends division. We'd much prefer to be Leaders than Legends. Tough luck, Yellow and Blue!

MICHIGAN

THE VICTORS

Sing along, if you must:

> *Now for a cheer they are here, triumphant!*
> *Here they come with banners flying,*
> *In stalwart step they're nighing,*
> *With shouts of vict'ry crying,*
> *We hurrah, hurrah, we greet you now,*
> *Hail!*
> *Far we their praises sing*
> *For the glory and fame they've bro't us*
> *Loud let the bells them ring*

continues

For here they come with banners flying
Here they come, Hurrah!
Hail! to the victors valiant
Hail! to the conqu'ring heroes
Hail! Hail! to Michigan
the leaders and best
Hail! to the victors valiant
Hail! to the conqu'ring heroes
Hail! Hail! to Michigan,
the champions of the West!
We cheer them again
We cheer and cheer again
For Michigan, we cheer for Michigan
We cheer with might and main
We cheer, cheer, cheer
With might and main we cheer!
Hail! to the victors valiant
Hail! to the conqu'ring heroes
Hail! Hail! to Michigan,
the champions of the West!

MICHIGAN

4
STORIES WE HATE

RIVALRY GAMES

ONE OF THE THINGS that makes Michigan football special is the rivalry games. Obviously, the Ohio State game is one of those, but it's a rivalry that was built out of years of competition, as opposed to, say, logistics or even a feud. And there isn't the exchange of an official trophy.

Michigan has two such rivalry, or trophy, games on its schedule. One is obvious—a yearly date with Michigan State, 60 miles up the road in East Lansing. The Wolverines and the Spartans play for the Paul Bunyan Trophy, which was commissioned in 1953 by then–Michigan governor Mennen Williams. Even though "little brother" has kept the trophy of the mythical woodsman for the last three years heading into the 2011 season, the Wolverines have won 67 and tied five of the 103 matchups with MSU.

But there would be no Paul Bunyan Trophy game—nor any other trophy games for any school, for that matter—if it weren't for Michigan, the University of Minnesota, an argument over water, and a little brown jug.

In 1903 Fielding Yost took his famed "Point-a-Minute" Michigan team to Minnesota with a 29-game winning streak in tow. Minnesota had one of its better teams that year, and the game drew quite of bit of fanfare and attention. When the Wolverines hit the field for the game, however, Yost realized his team didn't have anything to hold water for the players to drink. So he dispatched student-manager Thomas B. Roberts to find something, and Roberts went out and purchased the earthenware brown jug for 30 cents.

The Golden Gophers gave Yost's squad all they could handle that day, and when Minnesota scored a touchdown late in the second half that tied the score at 6–6, all hell broke loose. The partisan crowd stormed the field, and officials had difficulty in restoring order. The contest had to be called with two minutes remaining, and the game was declared a tie.

The morning after the game, a Minnesota custodian by the name of Oscar Munson found the jug (although some claim he stole it, which was never proven). Munson brought the jug to Gophers athletics director L.J. Cooke and, according to University of Minnesota archives, said to Cooke in his thick, Scandinavian accent, "Jost left his yug." Cooke decided to keep the jug and painted on its side: "Michigan Jug— Captured by Oscar, October 31, 1903," and the score, "Minnesota 6, Michigan 6." The Minnesota 6 was painted far larger than the Michigan 6.

In the meantime, Jost—er, Yost—realized he forgot the jug and wrote to Cooke, asking that it be returned. Cooke replied, "If you want it, you'll have to win it back."

Ironically, the two teams didn't play again until 1909, but Cooke and the Gophers proved to be men of their word— Michigan won the game and took home the jug as the spoils of victory, and they won again the following year. Ten more years would pass before the two teams played again, with Minnesota taking the prize in 1919. That began a streak of 80 consecutive games, broken only by the Big Ten's unbalanced schedule when the two teams did not meet in 1999 and 2000.

Of course, as far as the series goes, if Minnesota was looking to drink from the jug often, well, it would have died of thirst by now. The Wolverines lead this series 66–22–3.

BOB UFER

You can't hate Mee-chigan football without hating the man who broadcast 363 consecutive games from the radio booth in the press box from 1945 to 1981, Bob Ufer.

To Buckeye Nation, Ufer is as hated as Yost, Crisler, and Schembechler. His inimitable style, the unabashed, unapologetic love for Michigan that would draw criticism in today's world as being a "homer," the honking of the horn, and all the great "Uferisms" made Bob just as much a part of the program as the winged helmet.

Bob Ufer was Michigan—literally. He graduated from the University of Michigan in 1943, having played football as a

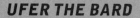

UFER THE BARD

After the historic upset victory over Ohio State in 1969, Ufer penned, and read on air, this poem:

It was November 22, 1969
That they came to bury Michigan, all dressed in maize and blue.
The words were said, the prayers were read and everybody cried,
But when they closed the coffin, there was someone else inside.
Oh they came to bury Michigan, but Michigan wasn't dead,
And when the game was over it was someone else instead.
Eleven Michigan Wolverines put on the gloves of gray,
And as the organ played "The Victors," they laid Woody Hayes away.

freshman but truly excelling in track, setting eight all-time Michigan varsity track records. His time of 48.1 seconds in the 440 at the 1942 Big Ten track meet was the world's best time in the quarter mile and stood for five years—and for 32 years as the Michigan school record.

It was only two years after graduating, in 1945, that Ufer began his radio career. What got lost in the blatant homerism and offbeat phrases that Ufer used—"Mee-chigan," Bo "General Patton" Schembechler, "cotton-pickin' maize-and-blue heart"—was the fact that he was a colorful announcer whose folksy manner painted a picture for those listening on the radio.

But the Uferisms and the calls made him famous. According to a beautifully written piece by author Garry Zonca that appeared in the Ohio State game program a month after Ufer's death in 1981, there were also these beauties:

> In 1969 he described Barry Pierson "Going down that mod sod like a penguin with a hot herring in his cummerbund."
>
> In 1975 Ufer talked about "that whirling dervish, Gordie Bell, who could run 15 minutes in a phone booth...and he wouldn't even touch the sides."
>
> In 1976 it was Russell Davis "running through that Buckeye line like a bull with a bee in his ear."
>
> In 1978 he said, "We're down in the snakepit at Ohio State and our Maize 'n' Blue dobbers are high right now cuz we're getting ready to do battle with Dr. StrangeHayes and his Scarlet and Gray Legions."
>
> And in 1979: "Johnny Wingin' Wangler and Anthony the Darter Carter combined for the greatest single play in the 100-year history of Michigan football"—the touchdown pass with no time left on the clock to beat Indiana.

Early in Schembechler's career as the Michigan coach, Ufer began using a horn in the broadcast booth whenever the Wolverines scored. Ufer said he got the horn from General George S. Patton's nephew, who was willed the horn by the great military man. The nephew was a Michigan fan who listened to Ufer's broadcast and knew that Ufer compared Schembechler to Patton. The nephew wrote to Ufer, asking him if he would like the horn that was on Patton's jeep. On the air, Ufer recounted the story and said, "Would I like it? Is the pope Catholic?"

The pronunciation of Mee-chigan, Ufer said, was a tribute to the great Fielding Yost. During Ufer's undergraduate days at U-M, while running track indoors, he would find himself wandering over to sit with the old coach—"I can see Yost now with that old felt hat on, chewing on his famous cigar—and reminisce with the former coach." Yost, Ufer said, had a decidedly southern accent coming from West Virginia and pronounced Michigan as Mee-chigan. "So down through the years on these Michigan football broadcasts, we kind of figured that if Fielding H. Yost could talk about his Mee-chigan, there wasn't anything with old Bob Ufer referring to it that way."

Ufer was so well-known, so well-loved among Wolverines, that he was asked by another Michigan graduate to be the keynote speaker for a rally. The graduate was Gerald R. Ford, who was announcing his kickoff rally for the Presidency.

In October of 1981, when it became clear that Ufer's days as Michigan's radio broadcaster were drawing to a close due to illness, the Michigan Marching Band spelled out U-F-E-R on the field. He died three weeks later.

5

COACHES WE HATE

BO KNOWS

TALK ABOUT IRONY. A man is born in Ohio, attends high school and college in Ohio, is an assistant coach in Ohio, and a head coach in Ohio. At the age of 40, he goes to Michigan to become the head coach of a football team. Twenty-one years later, he's "a Michigan man, through and through."

Well enough. As soon as Bo Schembechler's Mayflower moving van crossed the state line, he ceased being a Buckeye. The former Woody Hayes aide was a thorn in the side of all things Scarlet and Gray while he resided up north. Michigan was 11–9–1 against Ohio State during Schembechler's reign as head coach. But the Wolverines were just 5–12 in bowl games under Bo.

Glenn Edward Schembechler was born and raised in the Akron suburb of Barberton. Schembechler was a good but not great football player who attended Miami University in

Oxford, Ohio. He played tackle for one season under Hall of Fame coach Sid Gillman and two years under Hall of Fame coach Woody Hayes.

After graduation, Schembechler followed Hayes to Ohio State for his first coaching job. At the conclusion of a stint in the U.S. Army, Bo returned to coaching as an assistant at Presbyterian, Bowling Green, and Northwestern. He moved to Columbus as a full-time assistant from 1958 to 1962. Schembechler got his first head coaching job at Miami of Ohio and remained there for six years, compiling a record of 40–17–3. Following the 1968 season, Schembechler became the 15th head football coach in Michigan's history.

He retired from coaching at the age of 60, after a 17–10 loss to Southern Cal in the 1990 Rose Bowl. His final ledger: 194 wins, 48 losses, and five ties at Michigan with 13 Big Ten championships and a lifetime record of 234–65–8.

From 1990 to 1992, Schembechler left the world of college football and became the president of the Detroit Tigers. Bo returned to the Michigan campus in an unofficial capacity and was a regular on a local TV sports show. He represented the university at a number of functions and remained close to the football team. A day after delivering his annual pep talk prior to the U-M–OSU game in 2006, Bo died of heart disease. More than 20,000 mourners—including former OSU head coaches Earle Bruce and John Cooper and then head coach Jim Tressel and his entire staff—attended a service at Michigan Stadium. Schembechler was buried at Forest Hill Cemetery in Ann Arbor, making his "Michigan man" status everlasting.

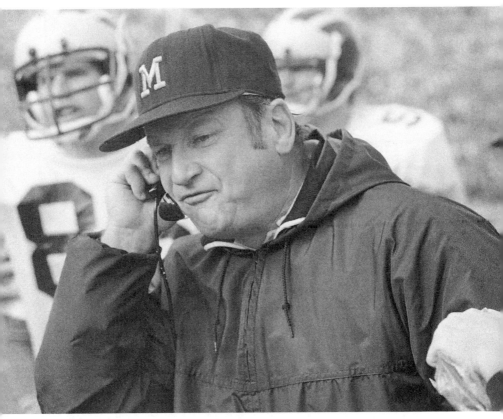

Bo Schembechler about to let fly with a few choice words during a game against Michigan State in 1977. Or perhaps he was deaing with a painful bowel obstruction?

DOES MICHIGAN HAVE A BO PROBLEM?

Glenn Edward Schembechler Jr.'s official bio claims that the name "Bo" came from his sister's attempt to say "brother" when both of them were young. That's a cute story, but...did you know that, in the medical profession, BO stands for bowel obstruction? Really. And in police reports, BO commonly refers to body odor. We're not making this stuff up.

MICHIGAN

13 BOs WE'D RATHER HAVE LUNCH WITH THAN BO SCHEMBECHLER

1. Bo Diddley—the Rock and Roll Hall of Famer was an innovator who got banned for life from appearing on *The Ed Sullivan Show* after he sang "Bo Diddley" when he was scheduled to sing "Sixteen Tons" during his first appearance.

2. Bo Jackson—the 1985 Heisman Trophy winner from Auburn was also a talented baseball player and the first person to earn in a spot in both MLB's All-Star Game and the NFL's Pro Bowl. He also was one of Nike's first celebrity spokespersons.

3. Bo Derek—the model-turned–film star was a 10-plus in the movie *Ten*. Even though there wasn't much more to her résumé, she could teach us how to put our hair in cornrows.

4. Bo Pelini—no-brainer. The former Buckeyes safety (1987–1990) is now the head coach at Nebraska. And he was named in honor of former Ohio State running back Bo Scott (who would be welcome to join us for lunch, too).

5. Bo Belinsky—the former big-league pitcher threw a no-hitter and married *Playboy* Playmate of the Year Jo Collins. That's a pretty impressive pair.

6. Bo Bice—the runner-up to Carrie Underwood in season four (2005) of *American Idol*. The man can sing, but obviously not as well as Underwood.

7. Bo Hopkins—actor who appeared in more than 100 films and TV shows, including *White Lightning* with Burt Reynolds and Ned Beatty.

8. Bo Outlaw—basketball star who played for four NBA teams from 1993 to 2007. His career .567 field-goal percentage is the ninth highest in the history of the NBA.

9. Bo Svenson—Swedish-American actor who played Joe Bob Priddy in the football flick *North Dallas Forty* and also appeared in *The Inglorious Bastards* (1977) and the non-remake *Inglourious Basterds* (2009). (Does that make him twice the bastard that Schembechler was?)

10. Bo Duke—John Schneider's character in *The Dukes of Hazzard*. Maybe he could bring Daisy Duke and Luke Duke to fill out the table. On second thought, maybe he can bring just Daisy.

11. Bo Brady—a fictional character on the TV soap *Days of Our Lives*. After getting hit on the head, he had psychic visions. He got hit on the head again and—poof!—no more visions. Maybe his psychic powers should have told him to look out.

12. Bo—the First Dog. The Obamas' Portuguese water dog might not be a great conversationalist, but he will certainly clean his plate.

13. Little Bo Peep—the shepherdess of nursery rhyme fame debuted in 1803 and is still going strong, despite the troubles with her flock.

MICHIGAN

MO MUST GO

As tough as it was to see a good Ohio man like Bo Schembechler leave the state, it was good for Ohio that Gary Moeller departed. Moeller is a native of Lima, Ohio, and played center and linebacker for Woody Hayes and the Buckeyes from 1961 to 1963. He was the team captain as a senior. Following his graduation, he began his coaching career at Bellefontaine High School in Ohio. Moeller joined Schembechler as an assistant coach at Miami of Ohio in 1967 and followed Bo to U-M in 1969.

Moeller was named head coach at the University of Illinois in 1976. In three seasons, the Illini were 6–24–3 (3–18–3 in the Big Ten) and never finished higher than ninth in the conference standings (back when there were only 10 teams in the Big Ten). In Champaign he is most remembered for leading the Illini to a 0–0 tie with Northwestern (back when Northwestern was the conference doormat, much as Michigan is today).

Moeller returned to U-M as an assistant coach in 1980, bided his time, and when Schembechler retired in 1990, Mo replaced Bo. In five seasons, Michigan was 44–13–3 under Moeller, winning three Big Ten titles. In that span, the Wolverines were 3–1–1 versus Ohio State and 4–1 in bowl games.

Moeller resigned in May 1995 after tapes were released of his drunken outburst following an arrest on charges of disorderly conduct and assault and battery at a suburban Detroit restaurant. Apparently, Moeller went on an alcohol-fueled rampage at the restaurant that included smashing glasses, singing loudly (probably a garbled version of "The Victors"), and attempting to dance with female patrons after his wife left to wait outside in their car. He also punched a cop as they dragged him away to have him tested for alcohol poisoning. Afterward, Moeller said, "I blew it, I just lost it, and now I have to live with it." This was a bit much, even by Michigan standards. When U-M athletics director Joe Roberson was asked if Moeller deserved a second chance, he replied, "Second chances are somewhat dependent on the circumstances that lost you your first chance. In my view, given what has happened, it would have been quite difficult for Gary to have been an effective leader of the team."

Moeller was quickly hired as an assistant coach by the Cincinnati Bengals of the NFL, then moved to the Detroit Lions in 1997. He was promoted to head coach of the Lions for the final seven games of the 2000 season and compiled a 4–3 mark, making him the first coach since Joe Schmidt (1967–1972) to compile a winning overall record for the hapless Lions. Prior to the 2001 season, Moeller was fired by new team president Matt Millen. He spent three more seasons as an NFL assistant before retiring.

LLOYD CARR
NICE GUYS DON'T FINISH LAST,
THEY JUST CAN'T BEAT APPALACHIAN STATE

What happened to Virginia? If the Cavaliers had been able to hold on to a 17–0 lead in Lloyd Carr's first game as Michigan's head coach in 1995, Carr figures he wouldn't have been the Wolverines coach for long. Carr's Wolverines won that game at Michigan Stadium 18–17, and the Wolverines closed out the

MICHIGAN'S SORRY BOWL GAME LEGACY

Having lost five of its last six bowl games, including most recently a 52–14 thumping at the hands of perennial powerhouse Mississippi State in the January 1, 2011, Gator Bowl, Michigan has taken its share of lumps in January. U-M's sad history also includes Bo Schembechler's seemingly unbeatable run of seven straight bowl losses from 1970 to 1979. You'd think Michigan would follow the Ivy League's example and just give it up.

	Won	Lost
Rose Bowl	8	12
Orange Bowl	1	1
Gator Bowl	1	2
Bluebonnet Bowl	1	0
Sugar Bowl	0	1
Holiday Bowl	1	1
Fiesta Bowl	1	0
Hall of Fame Bowl	2	0
Alamo Bowl	0	2
Citrus Bowl (Capital One)	3	1
Outback Bowl	1	1
Total	**19**	**21**

regular season with a 31–23 win against Ohio State to go 9–3 and earn a trip to the Alamo Bowl.

Carr had been bumped up to head coach only because Gary Moeller was ousted the previous May with his off-field problems. Most experts agreed that if Carr and the Wolverines didn't get off to a quick start, he'd probably be replaced. The following season, the Wolverines finished 8–4 but again beat the Buckeyes. Carr and Michigan made it three in a row in 1997 with a 20–14 win over the Buckeyes to complete an undefeated regular season. Michigan beat Washington State in the Rose Bowl to go 12–0 and win the national championship. In Carr's 13 years as Michigan's head coach, the Wolverines were 6–7 against the Buckeyes and 6–7 in bowl games. The Wolverines were 122–40 overall with five Big Ten titles.

Carr grew up in Riverview, Michigan, but played college football and baseball at the University of Missouri for three years before transferring to Northern Michigan to complete his eligibility. He began coaching at the high school level in 1968 and joined the Eastern Michigan staff in 1976. He was hired by Moeller at Illinois in 1978 and followed him to Michigan in 1980. Fifteen years later, Carr was named the head coach.

Carr's lowlights include: losing six of his final seven games against Ohio State, five of six bowl games from 2001 to 2006, and the team's home opener in his final season to Appalachian State. Yes, that Appalachian State.

BUMP ELLIOTT
COMING UP ROSES

Chalmers "Bump" Elliott holds the distinction of winning Big Ten championships at Michigan as both a player and head coach. Born in Michigan, he was raised in Illinois and played two seasons at Purdue before World War II interrupted his college career. When his stint in the military was complete, he enrolled at Michigan to join his brother, Pete, on the football team. The Elliotts, with Bump at halfback and Pete at quarterback, helped lead the Wolverines to an undefeated season in 1947.

Bump spent 10 years as an assistant coach at Oregon State, Iowa, and Michigan. He was named the Wolverines' head coach in 1959 and remained in that position through the 1968 season. His record at U-M was 51–42–2, and he won the Rose Bowl following the 1964 season. Against Ohio State, Elliott was 3–7. His final game as head coach was against the Buckeyes. When Ohio State scored a touchdown to go ahead 50–14 with 1:23 remaining, Woody Hayes ordered his offensive team to stay on the field and attempt a two-point conversion, which failed. When asked after the game why he went for two, Hayes answered, "Because we couldn't go for three."

Bo Schembechler was hired to replace Elliott, and the next season Michigan beat Ohio State. After the game, the team presented the game ball to Bump. Schembechler said, "I don't remember when I felt happier about anything in my life."

Elliott remained at Michigan as an associate athletics director for two years then was hired by Iowa to be its athletics director, a position he held from 1970 to 1991. When Iowa went to the Rose Bowl in 1982, it completed a rare quintuple crown. Elliott is believed to be the only person to have been with Rose Bowl teams in five capacities: player, assistant coach, head coach, assistant athletics director, and athletics director.

FIELDING YOST
WHAT WAS WRONG WITH OHIO WESLEYAN?

It was the first case of an Ohio football coach fleeing the Buckeye State to become the head coach at Michigan. Fielding Yost was the head football coach at Ohio Wesleyan in Delaware, Ohio, just 20 miles north of Columbus. (Who knew they had

Fielding Yost (right), pictured with Boss Weeks (left, with football) and Willie Heston (below), two members of his 1902 national championship team, which outscored its opponents 644–12, including the 86–0 whupping of Ohio State.

a football team, let alone that they could attract a future Hall of Famer?) It was 1897, and four years later Yost was named the head coach of the Wolverines. That was bad news for Ohio State.

Yost's teams were 16–3–1 against the Buckeyes from 1901 to 1923 and 1925 to 1926. Among the 16 wins were 12 shutouts. Yost's first team at Michigan went undefeated, outscoring its opponents 550–0, and winning the inaugural Rose Bowl. In

Yost's first four seasons, Michigan did not lose a game and was tied just once. In Yost's career, the Wolverines won six national titles and 85 percent of their games.

Chances are good that no one holding this book actually saw Yost stalk the sideline of an OSU–U-M game, but Yost's contributions to the University of Michigan specifically, and college football in general, are immense. And if Yost's Wolverines hadn't beaten the Buckeyes 86–0 in 1902, there might not be a "Carmen Ohio" (see page 117 of *I Love Ohio State*).

FRITZ CRISLER
WHERE IS HIS SEAT?

Okay, the next time you go to The Game at Michigan Stadium and you're one of 109,901 fans, please do something for us. Find the one empty seat in the stadium. Make note of the section, row, and seat number to solve the mystery that U-M's athletics department continues to perpetuate.

But first, the basics. Fritz Crisler was the Wolverines football coach from 1938 to 1947. He is credited with bringing the winged helmets to U-M, an idea that was stolen from Michigan State College (now MSU) by Crisler while he was at Princeton. Anyway, Crisler's Michigan teams were 71–16–3 from 1938 to 1947, including a record of 7–2–1 against the Buckeyes. His final squad went undefeated, won the Rose Bowl 49–0 over Southern Cal, and was voted the national champion. Crisler had become the school's athletics director in 1941, and following the 1947 season, he resigned as football coach to concentrate on his AD job.

MICHIGAN COACHES IN THE COLLEGE FOOTBALL HALL OF FAME

	Record	Years	Inducted
Fritz Crisler	71–16–3	1938–47	1954
George Little	6–2	1924	1955
Bo Schembechler	194–48–5	1969–89	1993
Tad Wieman	9–6–1	1927–28	1956
Fielding Yost	165–29–10	1901–23, 1925–26	1951

He remained the AD until 1968 and oversaw incredible growth throughout the school's athletics department. U-M's Crisler Arena is named in his honor. But, as we mentioned in "Traditions We Hate," the other honor he received was that, every time Michigan Stadium increases its seating, the capacity is listed as ending in "01," a tribute to Crisler, who made that request when he was AD. That one extra seat is for Crisler, forever. The exact location remains a secret. He died in 1982, so who's using the seat now? Need one ticket for the big game? Anyone, anyone?

BRADY HOKE
FRESH MEAT

Surprise, surprise. Another Michigan coach, another former Ohioan. Isn't Michigan tired of getting the Ohio castoffs? Brady Hoke is the son of John Hoke, who played for Woody Hayes at Miami of Ohio. Brady grew up in Kettering, Ohio,

MICHIGAN

TOP 10 THINGS HOKE WILL DO *IN* 2011

Brady Hoke appeared on *The Late Show* with David Letterman (a fellow Ball State alum) on December 8, 2008, to present a Top 10 List on Highlights of the Ball State Cardinals Football Season. Here's our Top 10 List on What Hoke Will Do His First Season at Michigan:

10. Expand Michigan Stadium's seating to 453,001 so that it will have its own Congressional seat, zip code, and 27 Little Caesars Pizza locations.

9. Have Michael Phelps work with Adidas to create a Michigan Speedo that the coaching staff can wear on the sideline on rainy days.

8. Get the band to stop playing "The Victors" and replace it with his favorite song, the theme from *The Brady Bunch*.

7. Use red numbers on the players' jerseys to show support of Michigan's state budget.

6. Hire Chris Webber as the team's timeout coordinator.

5. Schedule Southern Michigan, Middle Michigan, Michigan School of Dentistry, Michigan Bartenders School, Michigan School of Cosmetology, and the Detroit Driver's Ed School in an attempt to become bowl eligible.

4. Use Tom Brady as the team's long snapper during the New England Patriots' bye week.

3. Include a pictogram of how to tie a shoe on Denard Robinson's wristband.
2. Organize a Million Michigan Man March to Big Ten headquarters to protest Appalachian State's request to join the conference.
1. Pry Gary Moeller away from the Little Brown Jug long enough to make a team beer run.

MICHIGAN

and graduated from Fairmont East High School in 1977. He claims to have grown up cheering for the Wolverines, not the Buckeyes. He didn't get a chance to play for either. He enrolled at Ball State (known as David Letterman's alma mater, but not as a football school) and played linebacker for four years. He was captain of the team in 1980.

Hoke began his coaching career on the high school level in football-crazed Indiana, then moved to Grand Valley State, Western Michigan, Toledo, and Oregon State before landing at Michigan as an assistant coach in 1995. During his stint as a U-M assistant under Gary Moeller and Lloyd Carr, he was the defensive line coach, but he's credited with being the recruiter who landed Tom Brady. Said Hoke, "Tom wasn't the greatest athlete, with those skinny legs, but there was something about him."

Hoke stayed at Michigan until he took the head coaching job at his alma mater in 2003. His 2008 squad was 12–0 in the regular season and reached No. 12 in the national rankings. He fled Muncie, Indiana, after the season to take the head spot at San Diego State. Two seasons later, he fled SoCal for Ann Arbor.

HONORABLE MENTION: JOHN COOPER

It might be blasphemous to include an Ohio State coach in our list of coaches we hate. By all accounts, John Cooper is a good man. He was 111–43–4 at OSU from 1988 to 2000. But those weren't "Coo"s you heard from several sections of the stadium on many occasions.

More than his wins, Cooper will be remembered by Buckeyes fans as having a 3–8 record in bowl games, a 2–10–1 mark against Michigan, and never winning an outright Big Ten championship (although he did share three titles). Three times (1993, 1995, and 1996) Cooper's teams went into The Game undefeated and ranked among the nation's top five, but each time the Wolverines stunned the Buckeyes.

In 2008 Cooper was elected to the College Football Hall of Fame. He's yet to be inducted into the Buckeyes Hall of Fame.

6

WE HATE ANN ARBOR
AND THEIR FANS

THE UNIVERSITY OF MICHIGAN is split into three campuses in
Ann Arbor. Central Campus, where the bulk of the more than
30,000 students go to school, is considered the main campus. We certainly do not need to get into an aesthetics debate
between U-M's campus versus Ohio State. Suffice to say, Ohio
State's campus is steeped in history and is visually stunning
with its classical and gothic architecture. Michigan's campus
is also stunning—stunning that a "major" university could
have the look and feel of a third-rate horror movie.

Central Campus is the original location of the school after
the city of Ann Arbor donated and parceled off 16 acres of
land that were originally intended to house the state capitol
building. When state lawmakers decided to make Lansing the
seat of government in Michigan in a very intelligent move,
Ann Arbor officials instead offered the land to the university,

TOUGH CHOICE

If you had a choice, which would you prefer?

A. You have to wear a Michigan cap, shirt, and jacket (in clear view) every day for an entire football season; or
B. You never can wear Ohio State clothing (or scarlet and gray) the rest of your life?

which had been established in 1817 in Detroit. The University of Michigan accepted the offer and moved west to Ann Arbor in 1837.

From humble beginnings—Central Campus originally housed one school building, a dorm, and some housing for professors—came the campus we despise today. Central Campus is now the location of most schools of study, the exceptions being engineering; music, theater, and dance; art and design; and architecture and urban planning. Those studies are on the North Campus. Unlike Central Campus, which is right in the city of Ann Arbor proper, North Campus is a couple of minutes away and detached from the city. The master plan for North Campus and several of its buildings was designed in the 1950s by the vowel-heavy architect Eero Saarinen, who gained fame for designing the Gateway Arch in St. Louis and the TWA Terminal at John F. Kennedy International Airport in New York (and he brags about that?).

South Campus, of course, is the formal name for U-M's athletics campus. But Central Campus is where it's at.

Ten buildings on Central Campus were designed by noted Detroit-based architect Albert Kahn, including Hill Auditorium (which isn't on a hill) and the Burton Memorial Tower (which is really just an oversized alarm clock). The tower, 10 stories high with a clock on top, holds one of only 23 grand carillons in the world. The carillon weighs 43 tons and contains 55 bells. The tower is also put to practical use—it houses the university's school of music.

The Michigan Union was where President John F. Kennedy took to the concrete steps outside to announce the formation of the Peace Corps in 1961. Kennedy's successor, Lyndon B. Johnson, returned to U-M in 1965 to announce his "Great Society" program (and how did that turn out?).

And, what would a university be without its museums? There are several to choose from at U-M, from the expected to the offbeat. They include the Museum of Art, the Exhibit Museum of Natural History, the Kelsey Museum of Archaeology, Matthaei Botanical Gardens, the Museum of Anthropology, the Museum of Paleontology, the Museum of Zoology, and the Stearns Collection of Musical Instruments, among others.

Now, when the bulk of students go home in mid-May, it doesn't necessarily mean that the university and town shut down. Far from it. U-M engages in summer classes, like most other schools, and the city of Ann Arbor continues to be dull as the temperature goes up. Two major events happen during the summer. The Summer Festival, which celebrated its 28th anniversary in 2011, is a nearly month-long event from mid-June through early July at U-M's Power Center, Mendelssohn Theater, or Hill Auditorium. Those three venues host nationally and internationally known musicians and entertainers, while the parking garage next to the Power Center features nightly local talent and movies on the top floor, hence known as the "Top of the Park."

In addition, the city comes to a virtual standstill for four days in late July for the Ann Arbor Art Fairs, a series of five, separate juried art fairs that feature artist and retail booths on virtually every street in the downtown area and up toward Central Campus. Interestingly, though downtown Ann Arbor and the University of Michigan are separated by about a half-dozen blocks between Main Street and South State Street, they're two distinctly different cultures. The State Street area borders U-M's campus and is made up of typical student haunts—bars, clubs, bookstores, budget restaurants, Starbucks, ice cream places, and more. The Main Street area of downtown Ann Arbor is clearly more upscale, with high-end shops and restaurants (like Woolworth's and Denny's).

Among these downtown gems is The Earle. It serves French and Italian country cuisine in an elegant setting. The restaurant is literally underground—you enter the building through a set of glass doors and either walk or take an elevator one floor down. It reminds some of an old-fashioned speakeasy from the Prohibition era, especially with live jazz five nights a week, but as soon as you walk in the door, you'll get a jolt to remind you that this ain't Prohibition. There are walls filled with wine corks, and the The Earle's wine list is more than 1,000 bottles strong. The restaurant has received the *Wine Spectator* Best of Award of Excellence for 20 consecutive years. While it's certainly a great spot to bust the

University of Michigan students avoid stepping on the brass M on the Diag, in the middle of campus. It's considered bad luck, at least until you fail your first class, which won't be long after Hash Bash. Photo courtesy of Getty Images

MICHIGAN

U-Misms WE HATE

Of course, if you're going to walk the walk at Michigan, you need to talk the talk. Thanks to the human resource department at the university, here are some "U-Misms" that you need to know:

The Arb—nickname for the Nichols Arboretum, a 123-acre "living museum," featuring overlooks and trails through woods and fields, including a stroll along the Huron River.

The Arch—the archway through West Hall at the southeast corner of the Diag (see entry below), also known as the "Engineering Arch" (from days gone by when the College of Engineering was located on the U-M Central Campus).

Big Blues—the name campus bus drivers and many students use to refer to U-M buses that transport students from campus to campus.

The Brewery—a historic former brewery on Ann Arbor's north side, now home to several U-M departments.

Burlodge—the nickname for Bursley residence hall on North Campus.

The Cube—just to the north of the Michigan Union (in Regent's Plaza), a sculpture by artist Bernard Rosenthal. It literally is a gigantic cube, balanced—seemingly impossibly—on one point. You can spin it on its axis, although you need to be careful that it doesn't whip around and smack you in the head on the way around.

The Diag—the main part of Central Campus. Formerly a pasture, it is now a large area enclosed by campus buildings and still resembles a pasture.

The Dude—the James and Anne Duderstadt Center, formerly the Media Union, opened in 1996 as a special place to provide faculty and students with the tools and collaborative space for creating the future. Located on the University of Michigan North Campus, the Duderstadt Center houses the Art, Architecture, and Engineering Library, the College of Engineering Computer-Aided Engineering Network (CAEN), the Digital Media Commons, and the Millennium Project. The Mujo Cafe provides a space for refreshment and social interaction. It is named after the former U-M president and his wife.

The Fish—Ray Fisher Stadium, the home of Wolverines baseball.

The Fishbowl—the glassed-in area facing the Diag where Angell, Haven, and Mason Halls meet.

The Grad—the Harlan Hatcher Graduate Library.

The Half Ass—a cafe/hangout/music and poetry venue located in the lower level of the Residential College, also known as the Half-Way Inn.

The Hill—a part of Central Campus near the U-M Medical Center that features a cluster of residential dorms, including Couzens Hall, Alice Lloyd Hall, Mary Markley Hall, Mosher-Jordan Hall, Oxford Housing and Stockwell Hall.

MoJo—nickname for the Mosher-Jordan residence hall located in the Hill/Observatory area.

The MUG—the ground-floor food court in the Michigan Union.

Nat Sci—the Natural Science Building, designed by architect Albert Kahn and completed in 1915, which originally housed the departments of Botany, Geology, Mineralogy, Zoology, Psychology, and the School of Natural Resources.

continues

The Pringle—part of the U-M Medical School, the Basic Science Research Building Auditorium (located on Zina Pitcher Place), with its undulating, sloped roof is affectionately known around campus as Pringle Auditorium.

Stepping on the M—the brass M set in the center of the Diag was donated by the university's class of 1953. Ever since then, students have made a pastime out of not stepping on it. The most common superstition says that if you step on the M, you will fail your first exam at Michigan. Apparently, it's safe to trod on after that. (In a 1996 survey of U-M students, 56 percent wondered what that W in the ground in the middle of the Diag was for.)

The Toaster—this curved-cornered, black, and stainless steel edifice located on North Campus is home to the U-MHS North Campus Administrative Complex.

The U—shorthand for the University of Michigan.

budget or take an out-of-towner, The Earle remains a favorite of Ann Arbor locals and is certainly the only romantic, intimate spot in the city.

Ann Arbor also has one of the most vibrant musical scenes in the county (that's *county*, not country). Since the 1960s, the city has served as a launching pad for such well-known acts as Alice Cooper, Bob Seger and the Silver Bullet Band, George Clinton, and Iggy Pop, among others.

One of the best venues in the county for live acoustic music is the intimate setting of The Ark, a nonprofit organization that, according to its website, is "dedicated to the enrichment of the human spirit through the presentation, preservation, and encouragement of folk, roots, and ethnic music and related arts. The Ark provides a safe and welcoming atmo sphere for all people to listen to, learn about, perform, and share music." The Ark actually began in 1965 as a collaborative effort among four Ann Arbor churches that wanted to host a gathering place for students to hang out. As folk music was prevalent in 1965, it soon became part of the offerings of The Ark.

When the four churches decided in 1977 to no longer support The Ark, the board of directors decided to come up with a fund-raiser for the venue. The nationally known Ann Arbor Folk Festival was born and grew so large that it now uses U-M's Hill Auditorium for such well-known artists as Arlo Guthrie, Ani DiFranco, Roseanne Cash, and many, many more.

THE NAKED MILE

Here's an activity that hasn't taken off like many of Ann Arbor's perverted events. The idea for the Naked Mile was hatched by a group of U-M athletes in 1986. On a whim, they streaked across campus, and it's a race that has been on-again, off-again ever since. By 1999 hundreds of students were running down University Street, across the Diag, and into Regents Plaza, usually in April, at the end of the winter term. An official police report estimated the 1999 race drew a crowd of 10,000 gawkers.

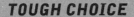
TOUGH CHOICE

If you had a choice, which would you prefer?

    A. Michigan goes 1–11 with its only win coming against Ohio State; or

    B. Michigan goes 11–1 with its only loss coming against Ohio State?

The University and Ann Arbor police began cracking down on the activity in 2000, citing safety concerns. In 2002 most of the participants wore underwear. In 2003 there were just five runners, and all of them were arrested. In 2004 an alternate route and an unscheduled day resulted in all 13 runners and one naked bicyclist escaping the long arm of the law. Then in 2005 the Naked Mile was replaced by the Painted Mile. Participants painted their bodies to conceal their nudity.

Slowly, interest in the race has returned. Even though only a couple dozen runners participated in January 2011, more than 7,000 spectators lined the course. When police officers arrested one of the runners, students began chanting obscenities. About 100 students formed a sit-in, blocking traffic on University for the rest of the night. Stay tuned and keep your pants on—or not. This is one activity that may not have run its course.

ANN ARBOR'S ANNUAL "HASH BASH"

One of Columbus' main drags is High Street. And you pronounce our great state: Oh, high. Oh! But at least Ohioans know right from bong—we mean *wrong*. It appears the

This is your brain on drugs.

MICHIGAN

TOP 10 U-M ALUMNI

The University of Michigan Alumni Association brags that there are 425,000 living alumni and notable graduates, including the "father" of the iPod, the founders of Sun Microsystems and Google, the first American to walk in space, the voice of Darth Vader, and a U.S. president.

Here are some other U-M alums and their activities that don't seem to make the Alumni Association's lists:

10. The aforementioned U.S. president, **Gerald R. Ford** (class of 1935)—pardoned the resigned-in-disgrace U.S. president Richard M. Nixon, who gave him the job.
9. **Dr. Harvey Crippen** (class of 1883)—killed his wife and buried her in his home's cellar.
8. **Richard A. Loeb** (class of 1922)—was arrested for the murder of a 14-year-old boy.
7. **John DeLorean** (class of 1957)—was caught in an FBI sting that led to his trial for federal fraud and racketeering charges related to funds he stole from DeLorean Motor Company.
6. **John List** (class of 1950)—murdered his mother, wife, and three children, left a written confession, then hid out for 18 years.
5. **John Buettner-Janusch** (class of 1957)—was convicted of making and selling LSD and meth and was sentenced to five years in prison. Later, he was charged with sending poisoned candy to the judge.

4. **Carolyn Warmus** (class of 1986)—was the key figure in the murder trial that became known as the "Fatal Attraction" case. She was accused of killing her lover's wife.

3. **Herman Webster Mudgett**, aka Dr. Henry Howard Holmes (class of 1884)—is believed to be the U.S.'s first serial killer. He confessed to 27 murders, many of them committed at a hotel he owned in Chicago, but authorities believed he was responsible for many more.

2. **Dr. Jack Kevorkian** (class of 1952)—known as "Dr. Death" for his role in assisted suicides. After being acquitted several times, he was convicted of second-degree murder and sent to prison.

1. **Ted Kaczynski** (class of 1964)—known as the "Unabomber" for sending bombs around the country, mostly to university faculty and airlines executives. He is currently spending life in prison without the possibility of parole.

MICHIGAN

degenerates in Ann Arbor do not. How else does one explain their annual Hash Bash festival?

The "festival" has taken place the first Saturday of April every year since 1972. That's the year the Michigan Supreme Court struck down a state law used to convict a local activist for possession of marijuana. Today, the City of Ann Arbor has very lenient laws concerning the possession of marijuana. It's just a $25 fine for the first offense, $50 for a second offense, and $100 for the third and all subsequent offenses. The charge is a civil infraction rather than a criminal offense. However, the State of Michigan has a bit stiffer penalty, and since the U-M campus is on state property, anyone caught with marijuana on school grounds faces higher fines.

But back to the festival. It's a collection of live music, street vendors, speeches, and a bit of civil disobedience centering on reforming local, state, and federal marijuana laws. The organization even has its own website. Not that you'd want to know, but it's www.hashbash.com. We refused to check it out, but one of our "creative" editors has the site bookmarked and tells us there are instructions for lighting up that day:

> No, it is not legal (yet) to smoke marijuana at the HASH BASH. The event takes place on the campus of the University of Michigan, and they enforce state law. But on city property it is not a crime, it is a civil infraction. Every year

TOUGH CHOICE

If you had a choice, which would you prefer?

A. You could never watch, listen to, or read anything about Ohio State for the rest of your life, but OSU wins the football national championship every year; or

B. You get to attend every Ohio State home and road football game for free for the rest of your life, but OSU never wins another game, and Michigan wins the national championship every year?

MICHIGAN

WEIRD MICHIGAN LAWS

Warning: crossing the Ohio-Michigan border can be dangerous and confusing. Consider these laws that are still on the books in Michigan:

- A woman isn't allowed to cut her hair without the permission of her husband.
- A man may not seduce and "debauch" an unmarried woman. Punishment is imprisonment of up to five years and a fine of up to $2,500.
- Any person over 12 years of age can receive a license for a handgun.
- You cannot kill a dog using a decompression chamber.
- People may not be drunk on trains.
- Dentists are officially classified as "mechanics."
- Chaining an alligator to a fire hydrant is prohibited.
- A woman may not lift her skirt more than six inches while walking through a mud puddle.
- In Detroit, it is illegal for couples to make love in an automobile unless the car is parked on the couple's property.
- In Detroit, willfully destroying one's radio is against the law.
- In Grand Haven, a person cannot throw an abandoned hoop skirt onto the sidewalk. Penalty: $5 for each offense.
- In Clawson, they passed a law that states it is okay for a farmer to sleep with his chickens, goats, horses, cows, and pigs.
- In Rochester, anyone appearing in public in a bathing suit must have it inspected by a police officer.
- In Port Huron, ambulances may not exceed the speed of 20 miles per hour.

the cops seem to nab a few folks during our ONE HOUR OF POWER! During 2002 the PO said they made four arrests during our ONE HOUR OF POWER, not that many for all the pot smoking that was going on…. The reality is there are more of us than them. They can't arrest us all! But seriously, BE COOL! Don't give the cops (crap), and they will probably leave you alone. These guys hate the paperwork. We do realize that some of you will come and as an act of civil disobedience LIGHT UP A BIG STINKY FAT ONE. While at this point we cannot endorse this, we can pass on some pointers to keep you from getting busted.

MICHIGAN FAN PAYBACK TIME

Okay, it's time to hear some of the jokes the people in Ann Arbor (the sick pukes) tell about Ohio State fans:

Q: How many Ohio State students does it take to change a light bulb?
A: One, but he gets three credits.

TOUGH CHOICE

MICHIGAN

If you had a choice, which would you prefer?

A. A high school football player from Columbus, Ohio, goes to Michigan and wins the Heisman Trophy four straight years; or
B. Your only child falls in love and marries someone serving a life sentence in prison?

TOUGH CHOICE

If you had a choice, which would you prefer?

A. Michigan wins the Big Ten football championship, but finishes last in the Big Ten standings in each of the other 24 men's and women's sports; or
B. Michigan finishes last in the Big Ten football standings, but finishes first in the Big Ten standings in each of the other 24 men's and women's sports?

MICHIGAN

Q: What does the average Ohio State football player get on his SAT?

A: Drool.

*   *   *

Q: You're stranded on a deserted island with three people: a cannibal, a mass murderer, and a guy in an Ohio State hat. You have a gun with only two bullets remaining. Whom do you shoot?

A: The Ohio State fan. Twice.

ACKNOWLEDGMENTS

MITCH ROGATZ AND TOM BAST at Triumph Books had the vision for this project, and, we have to assume, lacking any other viable author options, asked the two of us to take it on. We appreciate the opportunity, gents. Sincere thanks also to Adam Motin, our editor, who was forced to do the heavy lifting on this tome. Poor guy; with us, he never knew what was coming at him. —S.G. and D.R.

* * *

I also would like to thank my wife, Sally, and my daughters, Annie and Rachel. Thanks also to my 83-years-young father, Bob Greenberg, who also was our research assistant on this project. In 1963 Dad gave me the bug that turned into a full-blown Buckeyes virus, fueled more by this rivalry than any other factor. Shout-outs: to The Big O, whose work ethic rivals what Woody's was; to B, the best business partner a mogul could hope for; to Pearl for the best "*sonofadog*" rib-eye sandwich anywhere; and to Capt. Sparkmaster 5 of the s/v *shimeshay'n*, his crew and his trusty satellite dish. (There's nothing quite so satisfying as being afloat and watching the Buckeyes pummel another opponent.) And, last and certainly least, a big slice of appreciation to Michigan fans and players everywhere; thanks for being so...you. —S.G.

* * *

We owe a debt of gratitude to former Vice President Al Gore. Had he not "invented" the Internet, we would have had to break into and enter the local library under the cover of darkness long after closing time. That, as you might know, would have been against the law. —D.R.